brilliant

cover letters

brilliant

cover letters

What you need to know to write a
truly brilliant cover letter

James Innes

Prentice Hall
is an imprint of

Harlow, England • London • New York • Boston • San Francisco • Toronto • Sydney • Singapore • Hong Kong
Tokyo • Seoul • Taipei • New Delhi • Cape Town • Madrid • Mexico City • Amsterdam • Munich • Paris • Milan

PEARSON EDUCATION LIMITED
Edinburgh Gate
Harlow CM20 2JE
Tel: +44 (0)1279 623623
Fax: +44 (0)1279 431059
Website: www.pearsoned.co.uk

First published in Great Britain in 2009

© James Innes 2009

The right of James Innes to be identified as :   him
in accordance with the Copyright, Designs a

ISBN: 978-0-273-72463-6

British Library Cataloguing-in-Publication I
A catalogue record for this book is available

Library of Congress Cataloging-in-Publication Data
Innes, James, 1975-
  Brilliant cover letters : what you need to know to write a truly brilliant cover letter /
James Innes.
    p. cm.
  Includes bibliographical references and index.
  ISBN 978-0-273-72463-6 (pbk. : alk. paper) 1. Résumés (Employment) 2. Cover
letters.
I. Title.
  HF5383.I548 2009
  650.14'2--dc22
                2009027685

10 9 8 7 6 5
13 12 11

Typeset in 10/14pt Plantin by 3
Printed and bound in Great Britain by Henry Ling Limited, at the Dorset Press,
Dorchester, DT1 1HD

This book is dedicated to Graham. For breakfast with a glass of Fundador, for talk of underground houses, for his handbrake turns . . . For his eternal optimism and unflagging sense of humour, for his courage and his strength . . . And, most of all, for epitomising the entrepreneurial spirit.

Half of the author's royalties for this book will go to the Oxford Radcliffe Hospitals Charitable Funds (registered charity number 1057295), a charity which enhances facilities, services and research for patients and staff at one of Europe's largest academic acute care trusts. Major initiatives include the new Oxford Cancer Centre. I encourage my readers to join me in supporting this important cause. **One in three of us will suffer from some form of cancer in our lives**. Donations can be made online at www.justgiving.com/oxfordradcliffe

Contents

Acknowledgements

I would like to thank all of my colleagues and clients at The CV Centre, both present and past. Without them it would clearly not have been possible for me to write *Brilliant Cover Letters*. In particular, I would like to thank Susan Staley, who has closely supported me in the production of this book. I would also like to thank Amanda Jones, Katy Wilson and Nicola Staley.

I would additionally like to thank Richard Day at Beaufort Web Design for his significant contribution to the online elements of this book.

Special thanks also go to the team at Pearson, in particular Samantha Jackson, Caroline Jordan, Laura Blake, Lucy Blackmore and Kirsty Walford. I couldn't have had better publishers behind me. Assistance in checking and correcting the text was also provided by Don Elkins, Elisabeth Elkins and Malcolm Innes.

Finally, I would like to thank Delphine Vaucanson for her love and support and her toleration of my frequently working very excessively long hours!

Introduction

Dear Reader,

Why do some people almost always get the job they want?

Because *their* cover letter wins them an interview – and 99 per cent *don't*!

As a professional CV and cover letter writer, I see every single day which cover letters really achieve results. This puts me in a unique position, enabling me to bring you the very best of what I have learned – and helping you to create a truly brilliant cover letter.

Never underestimate a cover letter's importance

Cover letters are, according to a recent survey, seen by almost 50 per cent of recruiters as being equally as important as the CV itself, although most people spend the least amount of time on them.

So many people lose out on an interview not because of their CV but because of their cover letter. People are all too ready to blame their CV without giving a thought to their cover letter – and yet it's frequently the cover letter that is to blame for the lack of success.

When someone has hundreds of CVs to plough through, the cover letter sets the tone of the application, and should inspire the reader to turn over enthusiastically and read the accompanying CV.

It is the ideal opportunity for you to succinctly summarise and re-emphasise the skills and experiences you have highlighted in your CV, whilst also giving you greater latitude to express your personality. It can help to focus attention on your strengths and distract attention away from any weaker points.

Get it wrong and you may find that the recruiter doesn't even bother to read your CV. Applications can be rejected solely on the basis of the cover letter.

Consequently, I would strongly recommend you take your time in preparing your cover letter – and maximise your chances of getting through to the interview stage.

What can this book do to help you?

You're reading this book for one reason – to find out what makes a brilliant cover letter. Clearly, you already realise just how important a document your cover letter is and you recognise that getting it right can be tricky.

In *Brilliant Cover Letters* I aim to demonstrate exactly what you should and shouldn't do when writing your cover letters. I will help you to create cover letters that really work for you. This book condenses the same proven methodology I use every day with my clients and contains all the tips and – dare I say it – tricks that you need. I will cut through all the debate and opinion about cover letters and show you what really works from the recruiter's point of view – what I have *proved* to work.

Not only will we tackle the two main types of cover letter used in job hunting – speculative and advert-response letters – but we will also take a look at other letters you can use to boost your chances of success and achieve your goals.

The CV Centre website

I have made a commitment to readers of this book to provide numerous features online to complement the book, at The CV Centre's website: **www.ineedacv.co.uk**. On the website, I also provide you with the opportunity to make contact with me and my team directly. Features include:

- The CV Centre forum: You can exchange comments and ideas with other readers and also pose specific questions directly to members

of The CV Centre team, including myself:
http://www.ineedacv.co.uk/forum.

- The CV Centre blog: A regular column, drawing on specific questions, topics and problems raised in the forum and elaborating on them in detail: http://www.ineedacv.co.uk/blog
- The CV Centre tools: Free CV review, job vacancy database, templates download and so on.

As a reader of *Brilliant Cover Letters*, access to all these tools and facilities is free. Throughout the book you will be given special links taking you directly to the pages in question.

I have also prepared a special offer for you. If, after reading this book, you decide you would like one of our team to help further develop and perfect your cover letter, when you place an order with us we will throw in our CV Distribution service entirely for free.

With our extensive database of contacts, we can distribute your CV by email to a wide range of quality recruitment agencies and employers matching your requirements. Quite simply, the more people who see your CV, the better your chances of finding the right job.

Simply visit the following page on The CV Centre's site to take advantage of this exclusive offer: **http://www.ineedacv.co.uk/9780273724636**.

Thank you for choosing *Brilliant Cover Letters*. I have set out to write the most complete and up-to-date guide to cover letter writing on the market today – a definitive guide to cover letter writing. I trust you will both enjoy it and find it useful. And I look forward to meeting you on our forum should you have any further questions.

I really want to help you get the job – and the future – that you want.

Kind regards,

James Innes
Managing Director
The CV Centre

How to use this book

There's no doubt about it – this book covers a lot of ground.

However, I appreciate that you may well need to send your application off later today and simply don't have the time to read everything. I have therefore provided a 'fast track' below, listing the top 15 questions that people ask when writing a cover letter. This should help you to quickly and easily answer the vast majority of points that are troubling you.

Once you've found the answers to your questions, before finishing off your cover letter do make sure you spare five minutes to read the final chapter, Chapter 10: My five top tips to make your cover letter stand out. If you only have time to read one chapter of *Brilliant Cover Letters*, this is the chapter I would most like you to read. It encapsulates the most important principles that I cover in the book. Make an effort to accommodate all these when writing your cover letter and you'll immediately be well above average.

Brilliant Cover Letters brilliant case study

Writing a cover letter can be a lonely task. But you're not alone. There's someone I'd like to introduce you to . . .

Meet Joe Bloggs!

Throughout this book, I will be using a case study featuring Joe to illustrate the ideas and principles in question and to help bring them to life. This will also help you to better understand the issues raised and make it easier for you to apply the concepts to your own cover letter.

Look out for this icon:  **brilliant** case study

Everyone is different, of course, and there is no one individual to whom all ideas will apply. However, I have settled on an example that I hope the majority of readers will be able to readily identify with.

I won't tell you too much about Joe because we'll get to know him a lot better in the chapters to come. But, for now, I can tell you that he is 30 years old and works as a sales manager for a large stationery retailer, Stationary Stationers, following previous sales experience in the food and drink sector. He's now looking to continue on his current career path but, although he has just completed a BA (Hons.) in Marketing and Advertising, he feels that his opportunities are limited with his current employer. He's hoping that a move to a different employer will increase his level of responsibility and autonomy and, perhaps more importantly, increase his pay packet!

Besides the case study, I have included a variety of other example letters throughout the book. I'd suggest you take a close look at these. They should help you to generate ideas for your own letters.

The top 15 questions people ask about cover letters

Right, if you're short on time and need answers fast then this section is for you.

The chances are that you've got at least one – if not more – of the following questions on your mind.

I have compiled this list based on the questions we most frequently get asked at The CV Centre. It contains the top 15 most common questions concerned job hunters ask about cover letters – the questions that come up regularly every single day. If you're reading this book then it's more than likely that you will be asking yourself many of the same questions.

Each question is listed alongside details as to where in this book you can find the answers you are looking for.

All the answers to these questions and many more can be found within *Brilliant Cover Letters*. And if you have a question to which you can't find the answer then why not visit our online forum: **http://www.ineedacv.co.uk/forum**.

The top 15 questions

1 Which font do you recommend?
Chapter 1, page 16: Aesthetics and presentation: image is everything

2 How long should my cover letter be?
Chapter 1, page 34: Content and style: what to say and how to say it

3 How should I start my speculative/advert-response letter?
Chapter 2, page 41: The opening paragraph: capturing the reader's attention
Chapter 3, page 71: The opening paragraph: making an impact

4 How do I write a really compelling speculative letter?
Chapter 2, page 45: The central paragraphs: maintaining the reader's interest

5 How do I write a really compelling advert-response letter?
Chapter 3, page 73: The central paragraphs: stating your case

6 What should I do if an advert asks me to state my salary?
Chapter 3, page 81: The closing paragraph: including the salary question

7 How do I handle emailing or faxing my letter rather than just posting it?
Chapter 5: Digital considerations – email and fax

8 What possible pitfalls should I be trying to avoid?
Chapter 6: The 15 most common cover letter mistakes – and how to avoid them

9 Should I follow up on an application I've sent?
Chapter 7, page 125: Application follow-up letters

10 Is it a good idea to write a thank-you letter after an interview?
Chapter 7, page 129: Interview thank-you letters

11 How do I write a letter of resignation?
Chapter 7, page 146: Resignation letters

12 If I want to accept a job offer, how do I do this?
Chapter 7, page 150: Offer acceptance letters

13 How should I turn down an offer if I've got a better one?
Chapter 7, page 155: Rejecting an offer

14 Is there anything I can do if I get turned down for a job?
Chapter 7, page 158: Accepting rejection

15 What should I write if I want to request a pay rise/promotion?
Chapter 8, page 165: Pay rise request letters
Chapter 8, page 170: Promotion request letters

CHAPTER 1

Laying the foundations: getting the basics right

First things first: who are you writing to?

Obvious as it might seem, before you embark on writing your cover letter you first need to ascertain to whom exactly you are writing.

Getting through to the right person

The best person to address your cover letter to is clearly the person who is going to be making the decision as to whether or not to interview you. Too many letters are simply addressed generically to the HR Manager and start, 'Dear Sir/Madam'. You want to try to get right through to the decision maker.

This is an elementary sales tactic but, unless you work within sales yourself, you're unlikely to be aware of just how important it is to reach the person who actually has the power to make the decision you want them to make. It can make all the difference.

Not only do letters addressed to a specific person achieve better results (it quite simply gets their attention and creates a better impression), but letters that actually land on the decision maker's desk have an even higher chance of making the grade.

It may take some effort

If you're lucky you may have a job advert that clearly details to whom you should be writing. But not always . . . And it may take some effort on your part to track down the details you need – especially if you're working on a speculative application.

You may have to actually telephone the organisation to obtain the name of an appropriate contact. Trust me; it's worth it. A receptionist or switchboard operator will normally be pleased to help you out, but don't be afraid of asking to be put through to the department in question so that you can ask yourself.

Hiring decisions are often made either by the person to whom you would be reporting or by the person to whom they report – sometimes both. However, sometimes it is the HR department that makes the final decisions.

It's also worth looking on an organisation's website. Many organisations list their key personnel on their websites. (You should in any case be looking carefully at an organisation's website before you apply to them. Too many candidates know little or nothing about the organisation they are applying to.)

If all else fails

If all else fails and you are unable to obtain a precise contact name then letters can be addressed to either the Recruitment Manager or the HR (Human Resources) Manager. There's no reason why this shouldn't still elicit a response. But you might like to be a little more creative and take a guess at the appropriate job title of the decision maker. For example, if you are looking for work as a sales manager then the Sales Director might be a good choice. Even if there is no Sales Director, your letter should be passed on to the person who best fulfils that description.

Sending more than one copy

There's nothing, of course, to stop you sending in your letter both to the HR department and to the individual you believe to be in charge of your particular department (assuming you're not looking for work in the HR department!).

brilliant tip

Hedge your bets by sending in more than one copy of your letter and you stand even more chance of getting yourself noticed.

Understanding the reader's motives

Having hopefully established exactly who it is that you are writing to, you now need to try to understand what their motives are.

try to get inside your reader's head

Try to get inside your reader's head. Who are they and what do they really want?

There are three main categories of reader for a job application: HR personnel, managers/directors and specialist external recruiters.

Each of these types of reader will approach your cover letter from a different viewpoint. An HR professional will be trained to select 'best matches' between candidates and the person specification they have established for the role. A manager or director will be looking for someone they want to work with – someone they want to add to their team and whom they feel will make a significant contribution to that team. And an external recruitment consultant will be looking for someone they can successfully sell to their client.

If you can bear your reader in mind whilst writing your letter, it may make only a subtle difference to the way you phrase yourself – but it will be an important difference. Whether you're writing a letter, a report, an article or a book, it's always vital to establish who your audience is before you start.

Now that we've got this important question settled, we can move on in the next section to exactly how to structure your letter.

Structure: building your skeleton letter

All letters follow the same basic structure – the same basic skeleton into which you will place your content. In this section, we'll look at the key parts of this skeleton and how you should tackle them when building your own cover letter.

Letterheads

I would recommend that you start all your letters with a professional-looking letterhead. It is vital that the reader can spot, at a glance, not only your name but also precisely how to get in contact with you. Put your name (just your first name and last name) at the very top, followed by your key contact details – address, phone number, email address and so on. Place your address on one line, with your phone numbers on the next, and finish with your email address.

Problematic names

I regularly attend recruitment events promoting diversity in the workplace – events that naturally are also attended by a high proportion of individuals of various different ethnic origins. They often ask me questions along the lines of:

● What if your name is difficult for the average English speaker to pronounce?

● Do you have to state your 'official' name, i.e. as on your passport?

● If you're known by a shortened version of your name then is it acceptable to use that?

My answer to these questions is that you can – within the limits of common sense – call yourself more or less what you like on your letter. There are no legal restrictions, provided you're not attempting to defraud. If you use an alternative, abbreviated or 'anglicised' first name on a regular basis then there's no reason why you can't also use it on your letter – and on your CV. Changing your last name to a shortened version is equally acceptable. The key issue is not to hide your 'real' identity from a prospective employer. When the time comes to deal with contracts of employment you should make them fully aware of your full, official name.

Addresses

It is generally unnecessary to include UK county names in an address. Royal Mail approved addressing never uses these. However, it can be useful to include your county name if you are applying for work a long way from where you currently live (if, for example, you are planning to relocate), and you feel that the organisations to which you are sending your letters probably won't be able to work out where you are currently living from the name of your nearest town alone.

It should be noted that there is no need for a comma between city names and postcodes.

Telephone (and fax) numbers

Phone numbers should always include the local area code. The correct spacing (according to British Telecom) for London, Belfast, and so on is, for example, 020 7946 0000. For elsewhere an example would be 01632 960 960. This separates the code out and makes the remainder easier to read.

If you are stating more than one phone number then it's a good idea to specify what each number is – for example, 'Tel: 01632 960 960 (Home); 07700 900 900 (Mobile)'. If you're only including one number then there's no need.

 **brilliant** tip

> If you're based in one country and your prospective employer is based in another country, you should endeavour to include international dialling codes with your phone and fax numbers.

I would suggest you avoid using a work telephone number. Even if your current employer knows you are looking elsewhere and is happy for you to use your work telephone number for this purpose, your prospective employer doesn't know this and might think it indicates a lack of respect. A mobile number is normally very much better. It also gives any interested parties one single number on which they can reach you 24 hours a day, 7 days a week.

Email addresses

Whilst not having an email address at all on your letter is clearly a problem, it's not something I see very often. Far more common is the use of fun or jokey email addresses.

Whilst these may be fine for corresponding with friends and family, employers will probably regard more 'serious' email addresses as simply more professional.

Many recruiters report seeing applications with inappropriate email addresses – and this doesn't do the candidates any favours. Think about

think about what your email address says about you

what your email address says about you. Email addresses like sexylady@example.com and hunkyjoe@example.com or, getting really risqué here, mistressdominatrix@example.com and wickedandwild@example.com will clearly not help you present a professional image. (I haven't completely invented these email addresses; I have adapted them from real email addresses I've seen candidates use and have just changed them slightly to protect the innocent! Or not so innocent . . .)

You might have taken time to put together a brilliant cover letter, but if your email address is mrluvverman@example.com then it may harm your chances. I would suggest you open a new email account to use for professional purposes (e.g. Hotmail or Yahoo!) and keep your professional correspondence separate from your personal correspondence.

Convention dictates that email addresses should not be capitalised. Aesthetically it's probably more attractive to keep them in lower case anyway.

I'd also like to add that you should make sure that your email address doesn't appear as a 'hyperlink' in your letter, i.e. in blue, underlined text. Whilst this could arguably be useful in certain circumstances, it can also mean that the email address doesn't print properly to a black-and-white printer – and that is clearly a significant problem. In Microsoft Office you can remove a hyperlink by simply right-clicking on it and selecting 'Remove Hyperlink' from the menu that pops up.

Finally, I would suggest you avoid using a work email address, for the same reasons that you should avoid using a work telephone number. And if your current employer doesn't know you are looking elsewhere then don't forget that they are legally permitted to monitor all your use of their computer facilities. They're not paying you to hunt for another job!

---

brilliant case study

Joe's personal email address is smokinjoe@example.com, so he decided it would be best to open a new email account just for his professional correspondence: joebloggs@example.com. His finished letterhead looks like this:

JOE BLOGGS

1 Anyold Road, Guildford AN1 1CV
Telephone: 01632 960 314 (Home); 07700 900 159 (Mobile)
Email: joebloggs@example.com

The recipient's address

Following on from your letterhead you should list the name (including Mr., Mrs., etc.), job title, organisation name and address of the intended recipient of your letter. Unlike your own details, this should be listed line by line, although there is no need to include commas after each line; this is now considered 'old hat'.

Mr. James Innes
Managing Director
The CV Centre
Davidson Way
ROMFORD   RM7 0AZ

Incidentally, if you're not using the type of envelope through which the recipient's address can be seen (through a little plastic window), then you should use exactly this same form of address on the envelope.

Always take the time to check the recipient's address carefully – especially the postcode. It won't matter how brilliant your cover letter is if it never arrives!

Dates

The recipient's address should be followed by the date – and letters should always be dated with the date that you actually send them. This date should be written in full, rather than abbreviated – for example, 10 June 2009 instead of 10/06/09.

Dear …

If you've managed to obtain a contact name you should generally use 'Dear', followed by their title and last name – for example, 'Dear Mr. Hammond'. Don't use their first name, e.g. 'Dear John', unless they're a close acquaintance – and never use the format 'Dear Mr. John Hammond' or 'Dear John Hammond', under any circumstances.

Job titles such as 'Recruitment Manager' or 'HR Director' should only be used within the recipient's address. You should never start the letter, 'Dear HR Director'. If you don't know their name then the correct form of address is, 'Dear Sir/Madam'.

If you're absolutely sure of the gender of the individual, even if you don't know their actual name, then you could go with 'Dear Sir' or 'Dear Madam', but that can risk coming across as either sexist or overly politically correct, should your letter fall into the hands of someone else other than the intended recipient. A female HR manager might not take kindly to a letter addressed simply, 'Dear Sir', and you don't really want to alienate the recruiter with the first two words they see!

There is also the possibility that you're writing to someone whose official status requires what is known as a 'ceremonious' form of address – a member of the royal family, a peer of the realm and various other dignitaries. It's way beyond the scope of this book to list the numerous different ceremonious forms of address and, if you're writing to someone in such a position, I would advise you to consult a dictionary of English usage – or the Internet – to establish the correct approach.

Body copy

The main content of your letter comes next – and this will be the focus of the majority of this book. It will run from the subject line of your letter down to where you sign off with 'Yours . . .' and so on.

Yours . . .

Many people are unsure as to the correct etiquette for signing off a letter. It's clearly important to know the correct method, whether your prospective employer is a managing director, a professor of engineering or even Kylie Minogue! (Yes, I have had a client who wanted to work as Kylie's PA . . .)

Generally, you have a fairly straightforward choice between:

Yours sincerely,

and

Yours faithfully,

The rule is very simple. If you have started your letter with 'Dear Sir/Madam', then you should end it with 'Yours faithfully'. If, however, you have been able to start your letter with somebody's actual name, e.g. 'Dear Mr. Campbell', then you should end it, 'Yours sincerely'.

Even a letter to Kylie herself should begin with 'Dear Ms. Minogue', and conclude with 'Yours sincerely'.

The main exception to this rule is if you're on sufficiently friendly terms with the recipient to use their first name, e.g. 'Dear John', in which case you can end with 'Kind regards', 'Yours' or suchlike.

The other exception is, as I've already mentioned, if you're writing to someone whose official status requires a ceremonious form of address.

Signatures

After 'Yours ...' you should leave a few line-spaces before typing your name – so you can insert your signature afterwards.

 **brilliant** tip

> Make sure you leave enough room to fit your signature in without it appearing cramped. Four line-spaces is normally perfect, but at the end of the day it depends of course on how much space you've got to play with once you've finished the letter.

When signing, use black ink so it matches the rest of the ink on the page and won't cause problems if photocopied. For security reasons, avoid using the signature you normally use on official documents, such as cheques. In conjunction with the personal information you will be submitting with your application, your signature could be extremely useful if these documents were to fall into the hands of an identity fraudster.

The signatures people use at their bank are rarely very legible anyway. You should try to avoid the famously illegible 'executive' signature and aim for it to be easy to read your name from your signature.

Your name beneath your signature does not need to include your title (Mr., Mrs., etc.), and I would in fact avoid including it unless you feel it is necessary to clarify your gender to the reader. If it's not obvious from your first name what your gender is then there is certainly no harm in including your title so as to help clarify this point.

Enclosures

If you are enclosing other documents with your letter – for example, your CV – then it is standard practice to state this at the bottom of the cover letter. The accepted abbreviations are 'enc.' (or 'encl.') if there is only one enclosure or 'encs.' if there is more than one – for example:

enc.:   CV

Copies

In some circumstances you may be sending an identical copy of your letter to another individual or department. This should be acknowledged at the very bottom of the cover letter using the abbreviation 'cc:'. (This stands for 'carbon copy'. Although these days carbon paper is no longer used to make the copies, the expression has entered common usage with the meaning 'identical copy'.) For example:

cc: Geoffrey Winner, Head of Marketing

 case study

Putting it all together we get the following skeleton letter:

JOE BLOGGS

1 Anyold Road, Guildford AN1 1CV
Telephone: 01632 960 314 (Home); 07700 900 159 (Mobile)
Email: joebloggs@example.com

Mr. John Hammond
Sales Director
Boozy Direct Limited
Davidson Way
GUILDFORD   AN7 7CV

10 June 2009

Dear Mr. Hammond,

SENIOR SALES MANAGER VACANCY – REF. ABC123

Arma virumque cano, Troiae qui primus ab oris Italiam, fato profugus, Laviniaque venit litora, multum ille et terris iactatus et alto vi superum saevae memorem Iunonis ob iram; multa quoque et bello passus, dum conderet urbem, inferretque deos Latio, genus unde Latinum, Albanique patres, atque altae moenia Romae.

Musa, mihi causas memora, quo numine laeso, quidve dolens, regina deum tot volvere casus insignem pietate virum, tot adire labores impulerit. Tantaene animis caelestibus irae.

Urbs antiqua fuit, Tyrii tenuere coloni, Karthago, Italiam contra Tiberinaque longe ostia, dives opum studiisque asperrima belli; quam Iuno fertur terris magis omnibus unam posthabita coluisse Samo; hic illius arma, hic currus fuit; hoc regnum dea gentibus esse, si qua fata sinant, iam tum tenditque fovetque.

Progeniem sed enim Troiano a sanguine duci audierat, Tyrias olim quae verteret arces; hinc populum late regem belloque superbum venturum excidio Libyae: sic volvere Parcas.

Yours sincerely,

Joe Bloggs

enc.:   CV
cc: Geoffrey Winner, Head of Marketing

Aesthetics and presentation: image is everything

Presentation, presentation, presentation. Most jobseekers don't realise that the way their cover letter is presented can be as important in getting them to the next stage of the application process as the content of the letter. You will make an impression on the reader even before they read a single word. Presentation can make all the difference between success and failure.

> presentation can make all the difference between success and failure

If the presentation of the cover letter is thoroughly professional then the applicant immediately gives the impression of being thoroughly professional themselves. But the opposite also applies: a poorly presented cover letter will give a poor impression of you. Never forget that you are marketing yourself – and the way you present your cover letter can have an impact on the reader that is almost as powerful as the actual content.

However, it is rare for me to come across a cover letter that couldn't stand some improvement to its presentation and layout. There's normally always at least one area that can be 'tweaked' to improve its visual impact – and often several.

Why is presentation so important?

Good presentation can attract the recruiter to read through your cover letter instead of someone else's and will instantly give them a positive feeling about you. Conversely, poor presentation will build a negative impression of you before you have even had a chance to progress to the interview stage. Your application may simply end up in the bin.

Content is clearly more important – and we'll go into this in more detail in the next section – but aesthetics are also critical in making the right impact on the reader. First impressions are absolutely vital – and up to a quarter of job applications are immediately binned by recruiters because of poor presentation.

The key areas to address

To help you present yourself to the best of your ability I'm going to discuss in detail a number of key areas.

May I first of all say that I readily expect you will possibly be making the majority of your applications by email rather than by post – and any talk of paper choice or envelopes here is clearly going to be irrelevant when it comes to submitting your application electronically. However, at least for the time being, there are just as many (if not more) vacancies where you are still expected to apply by good old-fashioned snail mail.

We will in any case be talking more about emailing your application in Chapter 5: Digital considerations – email and fax. For now, let's assume you'll be sending your letters by post – and all of the example letters given in this book have been laid out on the basis that they are indeed being sent by post. However, as you will see in Chapter 5, it's very easy to adapt them to email format.

Choosing your paper

Your first decision will probably be what type of paper to use.

Make sure you use good quality A4 (no other size) paper that is not flimsy but not too thick either – 100gsm is ideal (80gsm is acceptable). White is fine. But slightly off-white (e.g. what is known as 'high white' – a very subtle cream effect) may be even better, because it adds a 'touch of class' that plain white paper lacks. It also sets your cover letter apart, because the majority of people still use plain white (also known as 'brilliant white').

You most certainly shouldn't use coloured or patterned paper.

---

brilliant blooper

There's a classic story of the candidate who (perhaps wanting to demonstrate that he had a sense of humour) submitted his application on 'Garfield the Cat' paper. If you're applying to work in a cat sanctuary and your prospective boss is a huge fan of Garfield then this might possibly give you an advantage. But in the other 99.9999 per cent of cases it certainly won't!

Printed or handwritten?

Unlike CVs, it is not unheard of for a recruiter to request that a letter be handwritten. This is naturally most likely for jobs where the quality of your handwriting is a relevant factor. Alternatively – and somewhat controversially – some employers will request this so that they can have your handwriting analysed by a professional graphologist, in the hope that it may reveal useful information about your character and personality. Don't be alarmed by this. There is, as it happens, very little scientific evidence to support this sort of analysis. However, if you are worried then further information can be found on The CV Centre's website: **http://www.ineedacv.co.uk/graphology**.

The best advice I can give is simply to take your time and to write neatly. You should be writing on plain paper, so try to place a sheet of lined paper underneath so that you can see through to the lines and use this to help you keep your writing straight and level.

Typeface and font

Assuming that you will indeed be word-processing your cover letter, here are a couple of quick definitions for you – because the key terms 'typeface' and 'font' are frequently conflated.

 **brilliant** definition

'Typeface'

A style of printed script, e.g. Times New Roman, Arial or Verdana.

'Font'

A subdivision of a typeface, e.g. Bold or Italic, including a denotation of size – traditionally measured in 'points'.

Note: These definitions are somewhat simplified but are more than sufficient for our purposes.

Typeface

I would strongly recommend that you remain conservative with your choice of typeface.

Presentation is, of course, a personal issue and some people will prefer certain typefaces to others – for example, teachers tend to like Comic Sans. However, it is important to realise that the easiest to read typefaces will get you the positive presentation points. We generally use mainstream typefaces such as Times New Roman and Arial, as they are professional, easy to read and get results. It is critical not to go over the top with fancy layouts, typefaces and so on. They can detract and confuse. A clear, conservative impression is always preferable, except in specific cases such as architecture, graphic design and so on, where you may be entitled to demonstrate a little more creative licence. But, in general, don't stray too far from the standards like Times New Roman or Arial.

Font

In terms of font, you need to consider the following.

- Bold. It's certainly acceptable to make use of bold type but it should be used sparingly – to highlight key points.
- Italic. If you want to highlight particular text in your letter then you should use bold, not italic. Italic, however, can – and should – be used if you need to quote the names of publications, i.e. books, newspapers, magazines, journals and so on. I wouldn't recommend using it for any other purpose.
- Size. Generally try to keep to 11 or 12 point. You can use 13 point or larger for your letterhead, but the main text should either be 11 or 12 point – and you should be consistent in your choice of font size throughout the letter.

brilliant tip

If you're going to be faxing your letter then don't drop below 12 point. Fax is not a perfect technology and some blurring is inevitable. If you use a point size below 12 then it can render your letter difficult to read. Rather than resort to reducing the point size, make an effort to edit your letter and to phrase it more concisely.

Colour

You should normally only use black ink. In certain cases it can be acceptable to make limited use of colour, but the general rule is to stick to black.

Your reader is expecting a black-and-white document, and whilst it can sometimes be good to stand out from the crowd, using colour to do so is not a technique I would generally recommend.

You may own a high quality colour laser printer with which to print your letter but, if you are emailing your letter to prospective recruiters, what sort of printers will they have? A letter containing colour may look very attractive on-screen but can lose a lot of its appeal when printed on a poor quality colour printer or, more likely, a standard office black-and-white printer. It is also often unsuitable for photocopying.

What is white space?

You need to carefully control your use of white space, presenting the information clearly and comprehensively – and with style – but within the limitations of the total space available.

'But, what is white space?' I hear you ask.

'White space' is a term often used by designers to designate those parts of a page that are 'left blank' (or, assuming you're using white paper, left white, i.e. not printed upon). Another commonly used and perhaps more meaningful term is 'empty space'. But I'm personally quite fond of the term 'breathing space', because that describes what white space is intended for – to give the reader some breathing space. It's not simply blank space; it's at least half of the document you are designing, and getting the right balance between white space and non-white (or 'positive') space is vital if you are to maximise read-ability.

The key to using white space effectively is to realise that its purpose is to provide 'breathing space' for the reader, so that they are not overwhelmed with a solid block of hard-to-read text.

brilliant tip

It's important to allow space around a letter for the reader to make notes. Not all recruiters will scribble all over your cover letter, but I, and many others, certainly will.

A letter with minimal white space generally comes across as cluttered and difficult to read – and this is definitely not going to help you get that job.

How to handle white space

White space principally involves your margins (top, bottom, left and right) and your use of line-spacing.

Spacing is – like all design issues – subjective, and a letter that might appear cramped to one person may appear too widely spaced to another. You should simply endeavour to strike a balance.

Margins

Keep them wide. They shouldn't drop below 1.5 cm, nor should they exceed 3 cm. 2–2.5 cm is perfect. When writing a letter, there is generally no need for either a Header or a Footer, so these can be eliminated.

Line-spacing

Whilst you should, in most cases, only leave single line-spaces between each paragraph, you may wish to insert additional line-spaces before and after the date so as to space your letter out to best fit the length of the page. You will also need to leave enough room for your signature at the end.

Justification

I recommend that the main text of your letter is 'fully justified'. This means that it is aligned to both the left and right margins, with extra space automatically added between words as necessary (like this book). It creates a nice, clean look along both the left and right sides of the page. This is easy to achieve with word-processing software.

Indentation

It used to be common for the first line of a paragraph to be indented. This is now considered old-fashioned and is no longer recommended.

Beyond the first page

If your letter runs to more than one page then it's a good idea for the text on the second page to start lower than that on the first. Given that you will be stapling the pages together, if the text on the second page starts too high up it'll be difficult to read because the staple will get in the way.

 **tip**

Whilst you should, in most cases, only leave single line-spaces between each paragraph, you may wish to insert additional line-spaces before and after the date line so as to space your letter out to best fit the length of the page.

 definition

'Readability'

Readability is defined as the ease with which a reader can absorb the meaning of your words. The more readable your writing is, the more effectively it will communicate to your reader. Research shows that working to ensure readability can have a positive impact on comprehension, retention and reading speed – and increases the chance that the reader will bother continuing to the end of the document.

> the more readable your writing is, the more effectively it will communicate

We have already talked about the importance of selecting appropriate typefaces and controlling your use of white space – both of which contribute to a highly readable document – but you might also consider using bullet points.

In case you're not sure what bullet points (also known as simply 'bullets') are, they're the small dots, squares, dashes and so on that can be used to introduce items in a list – for example:

- this is a bullet point;
- and so is this.

Some would argue that, in today's fast-paced world, recruiters no longer have the time to read large, solid blocks of prose. They need to extract the information they need – and they need to do it fast. Long paragraphs of prose are tiresome for a recruiter to read right through and, as a result, many simply won't bother. Bullet points, however, make it easier for the reader to take on board the key points at a glance.

Whilst I would definitely insist that you use bullet pointing in your CV, I don't believe it is necessarily desirable to use this when writing your cover letter. I would generally recommend you stick to writing in full prose. It is an opportunity to demonstrate your writing ability to the reader.

However, as always, there are exceptions to the rule. If your letter is lengthy and there are some ideas that are best communicated in list form then by all means use bullets. I'd recommend keeping it to a minimum though. Your cover letter is not intended to duplicate your CV.

Consistency of layout

The formatting you use for your letter should be consistent from beginning to end. Any inconsistencies should be carefully eliminated.

So many letters have errors in formatting. This can mean, for example, that some lines are indented more than others, some sections have more space between them than others and so on.

This just looks shoddy – and communicates a pretty poor impression to the reader. If you can't be bothered to take the time to perfect your letter then why should they be wasting their time reading it?

 **tip**

As well as consistency within the letter itself, it should go without saying that, if you are enclosing a CV with your letter (which you normally will be), both documents should match in style, ensuring a fully coordinated image. As the saying goes: 'Image is everything.'

Printing

In an ideal world, your cover letter would be printed using a high quality laser printer. Print quality does make a difference. If you don't have access to a laser printer then you should obviously try to use the best printer you can get your hands on.

If your letter runs to more than one page always print it on separate sheets. Never print on both sides, even if it's a high quality paper and doesn't show through.

Stapling

To staple or not to staple?

If your letter runs to more than one page then it is generally recommended to attach the pages to each other by placing a single staple in the top left-hand corner. Don't just paperclip or, even worse, send loose sheets.

Envelopes

When sending your cover letter (and CV) by post, I would definitely recommend choosing envelopes that match the paper these are printed on. A coordinated image can really impress. It is fair to say that in many cases the recruiter won't open the envelope themselves (and that the envelope will subsequently go straight in the bin), but, particularly in smaller organisations, they often will.

As for size, some people recommend A4 (known as 'C4' when it comes to envelopes) because this means you won't have to fold your letter (or CV). Personally, I am against this, because a large A4 envelope with just two or three sheets of paper inside is a lot more likely to get crushed, crumpled or otherwise damaged in transit. And using a hard-backed envelope is definitely overkill.

I would simply recommend the C5 size of envelope – equivalent to a sheet of A4 folded in half.

If you are sending your letter on its own without any accompanying documents, then I would suggest that the DL size of envelope is an even better choice. This size is the equivalent of an A4 sheet folded in three. Never use anything smaller than this.

↗ **brilliant** blooper

I have seen too many applications folded in four – or worse. It isn't an origami competition!

Some envelopes have little plastic windows through which the recipient's address can be seen. This can be useful but is certainly not essential.

Exceptions to the rules

There aren't many exceptions to the rules I've laid out in this section, but if you work within a highly creative and artistic field then you may be able to bend – or even break – some of the rules. I won't be giving any precise design tips – it's your field of expertise. However, I would warn you not to lose sight of the importance of readability.

Content and style: what to say and how to say it

It is, of course, extremely important to phrase your cover letter in such a way as to sell yourself as effectively as possible. You've got to hit the right note.

A cover letter is essentially a vehicle for you to elaborate on the relevant skills and experiences that are contained in your CV whilst allowing a recruiter to gain an insight into your personality (but not too much!).

Your style of writing should be formal and professional, but this doesn't mean it needs to sound stiff and starchy – quite the opposite. It should be written clearly, concisely, engagingly and articulately. Take your time over it; do not rush.

Action verbs

An effective way of making your cover letter have a greater impact is to make good use of what are commonly known as 'action verbs'. These are words such as:

- Accomplished
- Achieved
- Developed
- Implemented
- Improved
- Launched
- Managed
- Maximised
- Realised
- Strengthened

I have included a much more comprehensive list in Appendix A: 250 action verbs – just in case you are struggling to find the right word for your particular circumstances.

These words can be used to describe your skills and experiences in such a way as to emphasise what you have achieved rather than just what you did.

Choose your action verbs carefully so that they are as relevant as possible to the role for which you are applying.

The words in my list are all in the past tense. You can, of course, easily convert them to the present tense if you're writing about your current job, e.g. 'developed' becomes 'develop'. You can also use what is known as the present 'participle', e.g. 'developing'.

Positive adjectives

You will also want to use a good spread of positive adjectives to help reinforce your statements. Here are some examples:

- Consistent
- Efficient
- Experienced
- Innovative
- Positive
- Productive
- Proficient
- Resourceful
- Successful
- Versatile

I have included a much more comprehensive list in Appendix B: 50 positive adjectives.

Accompanying adverbs

I should also point out that many of these positive adjectives can be converted to adverbs where necessary, e.g. 'successful' becomes 'successfully', 'consistent' becomes 'consistently' and so on.

Avoiding repetition

Although it can be difficult, you should try hard to avoid repetition in your cover letter.

Preferably, you should avoid using the same adjective, adverb or action verb twice. Certainly, within any one paragraph, you should avoid using the same adjective, adverb or action verb twice.

Jargon

Feel free to highlight your knowledge and understanding of your work by using relevant terminology and 'buzzwords' – but this should not be overdone.

Excessive jargon is not recommended, particularly since applications may initially be reviewed by a central HR department whose staff may quite simply not understand a lot of the jargon specific to your role.

brilliant tip

If you need to use a specialist/technical term that you are not sure the reader will understand then it is perfectly acceptable to follow it with a brief definition in brackets. Do be careful not to insult the reader's intelligence though.

Numbers

Numbers often speak louder than words. Wherever possible you should aim to qualify your statements with specific figures if you really want to maximise the impact. Using qualifying adjectives like 'major', 'substantial' and 'significant' is all very well but do try to quote specific figures, percentages and so on. Don't just make a claim – back up that claim.

numbers often speak louder than words

For example, you could say:

I am currently directly responsible for supervising a regional team of sales executives.

However, it's always going to be more impressive to say:

I am currently directly responsible for supervising a regional team of 24 sales executives.

Always quantify where possible, whether it's simple figures, percentages or pound notes:

In my current role, I led the introduction of a major culture change in customer service, improving customer satisfaction ratings from 6.2 out of 10 to 8.3 out of 10.

I have been personally responsible for delivering the highest sales contribution for the group of 24.4%, with the closest rival delivering just 15.8%.

Most recently, I successfully tendered for a £2.3 million refurbishment project with a healthy 15% profit margin.

Publishing convention often dictates that the numbers one to nine be written out in full in text, whereas figures should be used for any number higher than that. For example, you can say 314 but you have to spell out seven. This convention is fine for general publishing and is commonly observed in books, magazines and newspapers. However, your cover letter is not a normal piece of writing; it is a marketing document – and, in marketing, the normal rules don't necessarily apply. I would personally recommend quoting all numbers in figures rather than letters because they're a lot more eye-catching that way and are likely to achieve a greater impact.

Percentages

It is also a common publishing convention for the symbol % to be written as 'per cent'. Again, I would advise against this for the same reasons. A % symbol takes up less space and yet has greater visual impact.

Money, money, money

When it comes to specifying quantities of money, it is accepted practice to abbreviate thousands to the letter K, e.g. £45,000 to £45K. Millions can be similarly abbreviated, e.g. £2.3M, but this is less common and I personally feel that, in this particular case, the full word, 'million' has more psychological impact.

Avoiding I-strain

The word 'I' is often overused in cover letters. Unlike a CV, a cover letter should of course be written in the first person. However, if you start every sentence with 'I' then it can make for pretty tedious reading.

You also risk conveying an impression of arrogance and egocentrism: 'I this . . .', 'I that . . .', 'I the other . . .', 'me, me, me!'

It might not be easy to cut down on your use of 'I', but you should definitely make an effort to do so. Look at each sentence that begins with 'I' and see whether you can rephrase it so that it starts with a different word.

If you can turn round a sentence so that it starts with 'You' or 'Your' then this is ideal, because it shows your focus is on the reader, not on yourself.

Spelling, typos and punctuation

↗ brilliant statistic

Sixty per cent of CVs and cover letters contain at least one linguistic error.

For documents that are supposed to be perfect, that's a fairly staggering proportion, isn't it?

It is impossible to stress enough how important this issue is. Spelling and grammatical errors are amongst the most irritating errors a recruiter sees, amongst the most damaging errors you can make – and are also amongst the most easily avoided. The answer is to check, check and check again – and then have someone else check for good measure.

Reading through your cover letter yourself is clearly essential, but having a friend or colleague read through it can be an even better idea – because it's so easy to miss mistakes in your own work when you've been staring at it for hours.

Spelling

Spelling errors can make a huge difference to your career prospects.

In one unfortunate case, the individual in question got very confused about the difference between 'role' and 'roll'. He kept referring throughout both his cover letter and his CV to the various 'rolls' he had had – for example, 'an important roll in the finance department', 'sharing a roll with another colleague' and so on.

Another interesting example was the receptionist who spent all day receiving and transmitting massages!

Any word can be misspelled, even 'misspelled' itself! However, some words are very frequently misspelled in cover letters and these are the ones you should keep a particularly careful eye out for:

- separate – often seen spelled as 'seperate';
- necessary – neccesary, necessery, nesessary;
- liaising – most commonly misspelled as 'liasing';
- liaison – likewise misspelled as 'liason';
- personnel – personnell, personell, personel.

Easily confused words

There are also various 'pairs' of words that I commonly see used incorrectly in cover letters, which I'd like to draw to your attention. It can be a little complicated so, if you get at all confused, I suggest you get out the dictionary!

- principle/principal

'The principal problem you might face with a new project is that you don't agree, in principle, with the approach the management wants you to take.'

'Principle' is a noun, commonly referring to a personal belief or conviction, e.g. 'It's against my principles.' Alternatively it can refer to how something works, e.g. 'The principle of a hot air balloon is very simple.'

'Principal', however, can be both an adjective and a noun. As an adjective, it normally means first, main or chief, e.g. 'My principal objection is the cost.' As a noun, however, it has a whole host of different meanings.

● stationery/stationary

'You might be responsible for ordering stationery supplies from the stationer. However, if you're stuck in your car at the traffic lights then you're stationary!'

'Stationery' is a noun for writing materials – paper, pens and so on. 'Stationary' is an adjective that means standing still or not moving.

● arise/arouse

'A rude and abusive call centre worker could easily cause customer complaints to arise – and that might arouse a rather angry response from the management.'

These two words have distinctly different meanings.

⚹ brilliant blooper

'I was tasked with handling and swiftly resolving any customer complaints which might arouse.'

● effect/affect

'You can effect a change and, depending on the circumstances, you can also affect a change. However, whilst a change will have an effect, it can't have an affect. And, whilst you might be affected by a change, you certainly can't be effected by it.'

This is a complicated one!

● advice/advise

'You might advise your clients not to sue the local newspaper, but they might decide to totally ignore your advice.'

'Advice' is a noun and 'advise' is a verb. They're not only different words, but they're also pronounced differently.

● practice/practise

'You can work in a doctor's practice and you can put your ideas into practice, but if you want to deliver an outstanding presentation to a potential client then you had better practise!'

Whilst pronounced the same, 'practice' is a noun and 'practise' is a verb.

In American English, 'practise' doesn't actually exist at all. Americans use 'practice' both as a noun and as a verb and this is just one of many differences between British English and American English.

Let's take a closer look at the vagaries of our American cousins.

Across the pond . . .
The differences between British English and American English are numerous and often cause confusion. The bottom line is that if you're looking for work in the UK, clearly you should be using British English spelling.

We've covered 'practice'/'practise'. Here's another problematic pair:

● licence/license

'Licence' is a noun in British English and 'license' is a verb. A driving examiner can license you to drive – but the plastic card you'll get is your licence. Americans, on the other hand, don't use the word 'licence' at all. They use 'license' both as a noun and as a verb.

A particular problem is that word-processing software (for example, Microsoft Word) is often, by default, set to American spelling rather than British English (because the software creators are normally American). It will therefore highlight some words as incorrect even when they're not – they're just British English spellings and not American spellings. This can often be resolved by ensuring that the document is set to UK spelling.

brilliant tip

In Microsoft Word 2007:

- open your cover letter;
- select the entire document by pressing Control and A;
- click on the language bar at the bottom of the screen (next to the Page and Word counts);
- select English (United Kingdom);
- click the Default button and then 'Yes' so as to update your 'Normal' template (as Word likes to call it);
- click OK.

The procedure in Microsoft Word 2000/2003 is very similar, except that there isn't a language bar. Instead you will need to go to Tools, then Language and then across to Set Language. Also, the language will be referred to as 'English U.K.' rather than 'English (United Kingdom)'.

For other-word processing packages you can consult the user guide or use the built-in 'Help' facility. Failing that, you can find the solution online.

Typos

'Typos' or typographical errors can be even harder to pick up on than plain spelling errors. A spell check won't pick up on mistakes such as 'working in a busty office'! You may be surprised, but this sort of error is not unusual. Take a look at where the letters 't' and 'y' sit on a keyboard – right next to each other. It's very easy to try to hit a 'y' and get a 'ty' instead.

As well as adding in an extra letter, another common typo is to miss out a letter completely: 'I worked closely with the Finance Manger.'

I've certainly seen some interesting job titles ... I had one client who was a Metal Health Advisor and another who was looking for work as a Diary Farmer!

It is essential not only to run a spell check through the finished letter but also to proofread it carefully.

And it's not just words – it can be numbers too:

I successfully completed my BA (Hons.) English Literature in 1888.

That's rather a long time ago!

Superfluous spaces

You should also be careful to eliminate all superfluous spaces between words – for example, 'eliminate   superfluous spaces' has two spaces between 'eliminate' and 'superfluous'.

Word-processing software will often, depending on what type and settings you've got, help you by highlighting such errors (often with green underlining).

Freudian slips

A final type of spelling/typing error I'd like to cover is where the writer, for whatever reason, simply picks the wrong word.

These can be of the banal sort where you type 'their' instead of 'there' or 'your' instead of 'you're'. You know which is correct but your brain somehow sends a different message to the keyboard.

Alternatively, typos can be rather more interesting. One which immediately springs to my mind is the hopeful jobseeker who stated they were 'a conscious employee'. You'd hope so, really ...

Probably one of the best typos I've seen was a candidate explaining that they were 'financially incompetent'!

You probably think I'm making all of this up but, trust me, it wouldn't be in this book if I hadn't actually seen it.

A spell check won't detect these sorts of problem – but a prospective employer very possibly will. Again, careful proofreading is the answer.

Punctuation

Errors in punctuation are the most common grammatical errors and, amongst these, the apostrophe is definitely the most abused. For example:

Londons' No. 1 retailer of kitchen appliances

Or, possibly even worse:

Londons No. 1 retailer of kitchen appliances

The correct usage is, of course:

London's No. 1 retailer of kitchen appliances

If you're not sure what the rules are then there are plenty of articles on the Internet that explain correct punctuation in detail.

It's and *its* are also frequently misused. And you sometimes even see *its'* – which doesn't exist at all!

Remember that '*it's*' is a contraction of '*it is*' (or '*it has*') whereas '*its*' is a possessive pronoun – for example, 'When it's necessary, the computer will automatically update its anti-virus software.'

Poor old apostrophes – so frequently mistreated.

It's not always black and white, of course. Whilst it is grammatically correct to say 'four years' experience', we find a lot of our clients initially complain when we do this, thinking it's an error. Many people assume it should be 'four year's experience'. You might fear (and reasonably so) that a recruiter may also think it is a mistake and so it is better for you to make a deliberate error. The choice is yours. This is the only time I would ever consider recommending anything less than grammatical perfection.

Can you spot any spelling, grammatical or typographical errors in this book? We hope not! But, if you do, then please visit **http://www.ineedacv.co.uk/oops** to let us know so that we can correct it for the next edition.

Length

As a general rule, most cover letters don't – and shouldn't – exceed one A4 page in length. Never lose sight of the fact that your cover letter is not intended to take the place of your CV – it's meant to act as an introduction.

keep your letters short and sweet

Unless there are clear instructions to the contrary, you should aim to keep your letters short and sweet. A handful of paragraphs are normally more than sufficient to whet the recruiter's appetite and entice them to read your CV.

If you find your letter is spilling over on to a second page then you need to take a long, hard look at what you've written and consider:

● finding ways to communicate the same points more concisely;

● ruthlessly eliminating all unnecessary words and phrases;

● removing some of the less important points you've made.

As with all rules, there are exceptions. For vacancies with particularly complex requirements it may simply not be possible to fit all that you wish to say on to a single A4 sheet. This may well be the case for medical or academic roles. It is also very common within the teaching profession for a cover letter to run to two pages. We'll cover so-called 'letters of application' in Chapter 4: Specialist cover letters – including letters of application.

Regardless of the line of work, a recruiter may sometimes (for whatever reason) stipulate a specific length of letter required, and you should of course endeavour to adhere to such instructions.

Tailor your application

In just the same way that your CV should ideally be tailored for each application, so should your cover letter. In fact, it is even more important to tailor your letter. A carefully targeted letter can easily mean the difference between success and failure.

It is astonishing how many people use exactly the same cover letter and exactly the same CV for every single application.

It stands to reason that every job and every organisation is different and every cover letter should therefore also be subtly different. If you send the same letter to everyone, changing only a few minor details such as the recipient's name and address, then your chances of success will most definitely fall considerably.

Nobody likes being spammed.

A recruiter's task is to identify the best matches between vacancies and candidates. They're not looking to find you the job that is best suited to you. They're looking to find the candidate that is best suited to them – so you need to approach each of your letters from the recruiter's perspective.

Instead of taking your skills and experience as the starting point, your starting point needs to be the requirements of the job you are seeking or the advertised vacancy in question.

Whether you're writing a speculative letter or an advert-response letter, you need to make it clear to the reader that you are writing to them personally, that you have made the effort to carefully analyse their needs and that you really do want to work for their organisation in particular.

Generic cover letters don't work; specific, carefully tailored and highly targeted cover letters are the ones that achieve results.

Summary

- If you can bear your reader in mind whilst writing your letter it will make a subtle – but important – difference to the way you phrase yourself.
- The way your letter is presented can be as important in getting to

the next stage of the application process as its content. First impressions are absolutely vital.

- Your cover letter should be written clearly, concisely, engagingly and articulately. Take your time over it; do not rush.

- Never lose sight of the fact that your cover letter is not intended to take the place of your CV; it's meant to act as an introduction.

- Generic cover letters don't work; specific, carefully tailored and highly targeted cover letters are the ones that achieve results.

CHAPTER 2

Speculative letters: getting your foot in the door

Basic principles

I believe speculative applications to be of much greater importance in a job hunt than most people give them credit for.

It may sound a long shot – and I'll admit that you probably will have a relatively low level of response – but if you have put together a strong CV and cover letter (the cover letter being particularly important) then you really are in with a chance.

Nothing ventured, nothing gained!

The hidden job market

Do you know how much an employer has to pay to advertise a vacancy in a national newspaper? And how much do you think a recruitment agency normally charges? Believe me, it's a lot of money. Any employer in their right mind will be keen to avoid such costs if it's practical to do so.

More than half of all job vacancies are never advertised or put out to recruitment consultants. That's an awful lot of jobs! These positions are filled:

- by employers trawling through their files for CVs;
- via word of mouth;
- through network contacts;
- by 'poaching' from other organisations.

It's the first item on that list that you're most interested in. When a position comes up, you want to make sure that your CV is in that all-important file – and hasn't just been chucked in the bin the moment it was received. And the cover letter you write can make all the difference.

brilliant tip

Even though an employer may not have any vacancies at the time of your initial application, they may well do so in the near future. As long as your CV and cover letter make a powerful impression, you should hopefully be considered when a suitable position does arise.

You may still find yourself up against candidates supplied by a recruitment agency, but the fact that you can essentially be recruited 'for free' may be a deciding factor, particularly for a small company. I hired my first ever employee after she wrote to me out of the blue on a purely speculative basis – and I've hired many more in this way since.

Finding your targets

Identifying suitable targets for speculative applications will require some research on your part, but local (and even national) newspapers, *Yellow Pages* and the Internet are generally the best places to start. Trade journals can also be very useful, not least because of the additional background information they can sometimes provide. However, having identified a target, it's not usually too difficult to dig up relevant information online – information you can use when crafting your cover letter. The Internet is a wonderful research tool. (I'll talk more about finding and researching appropriate targets in Chapter 9, page 189: Job hunting.)

You also need to try to ascertain what sorts of individual these organisations are likely to be looking for. The more you know about the kind of person they employ, the better able you will be to deliver what it is they are looking for. You need to identify what particular skills and qualifications are likely to be of most interest to them. This sort of research will clearly help you to strengthen the impact of your speculative application.

There is a case to be made for sending as many applications as possible, on the basis that this might increase your overall chances. However, if you send applications to organisations that aren't appropriate then you are simply wasting both your time and theirs – and potentially tarnishing your reputation. You will also inevitably spend less time tailoring each individual application. It is undoubtedly better to target a smaller number of organisations and to really take the time to understand their needs and to address them.

 **case study**

Joe Bloggs has decided to write speculative letters to a number of appropriate companies in and around his home town of Guildford. We'll see throughout the rest of the chapter how he crafts his cover letters so that they have the best possible chance of achieving the desired response.

The opening paragraph: capturing the reader's attention

make sure you capture the reader's attention right from the very start

The primary goal of your opening paragraph is, of course, to explain to the reader why it is that you are writing to them. However, your secondary goal should be to make sure you capture the reader's attention right from the very start.

If you're writing a speculative letter then the reason you're writing is to enquire about any positions that might be available – either now or possibly in the future. But how do you do this so as to get the reader's interest? You need to answer four questions that will be on the recruiter's mind:

● Why are you interested in working for them?

- What role is it that you are looking for?
- What are you offering them?
- Why should they care?!

Finding your 'hook'

Ideally you should be able to conjure up some kind of excuse (I prefer the sales term, a 'hook') to explain why you are particularly interested in them and their organisation.

- Maybe there has been a recent piece about the organisation in the press.
- Perhaps you have heard the company has just won a major new contract.
- Maybe you've heard they are relocating or moving to larger premises.
- Possibly they're launching a new product or service.
- Perhaps they have just released their annual accounts and reports.
- Perhaps they're currently participating in a major event, exhibition, fair or conference.

brilliant tip

Whilst hunting for a new job you should always be on the lookout for suitable 'hooks' you can use to your advantage.

Another possibility is that you've been given their details by a mutual contact. If this is the case then make sure you say so right at the very start of your letter. You stand a much better chance of encouraging the recipient to read further if you can add this kind of personal touch to the letter.

You're simply looking for something that will make your letter stand out immediately from all the other letters they'll be receiving.

Don't lose them with your opening words

Either your opening words grab the reader's attention or they don't. The reader hasn't asked you to send them a letter so why should they bother reading it? That may sound harsh, but it is the reality of the situation.

Don't waste your time – and theirs – by churning out a bland and uninspiring introduction:

I am writing to enquire whether you have any vacancies within your organisation . . .

Cut straight to the chase. You can't afford to lose the reader's attention with your opening words.

Deploy your 'hook' and immediately follow it up with a – brief – summary of what it is that you are offering and why that should be of interest to them.

⤴ brilliant case study

Having previously worked within the food and drink sector, Joe subscribes to *The Grocer* magazine. In the latest issue he has read an interesting article that has given him an idea for a company to which he can send a speculative letter:

> Having recently seen the article in *The Grocer* mentioning the impressive new warehousing facility you are constructing in Guildford, I am writing to outline my extensive experience and successful track record as a Sales Manager. I believe I possess the skills, qualifications and vital experience necessary to make a very significant contribution to your sales operation.

Remember those four questions that will be on the reader's mind. Joe has successfully answered all four of them in just two sentences.

- He's interested in working for them because he's heard about their impressive new warehouse facility being built in his home town.
- He's looking for a role in sales, probably as a sales manager.
- He's offering them extensive experience and a successful track record in this field.

- This is important to them because he could make a very significant contribution to their own sales operation.

What if you don't have a hook?

What if you don't have any specific reason to write to an organisation? You might have just plucked their details from the *Yellow Pages*. The majority of speculative letters don't have any sort of 'hook', but this is nothing to worry about. It's certainly not always possible to find a hook and, whilst having a hook may put you at an advantage, you can still construct your letter without one. You just need to substitute it with a suitable answer to that first – and most critical – question: 'Why are you interested in working for them?'

 **case study**

Joe has used his local knowledge to draw up a short list of local companies he feels may be interested in his services as a sales manager. There's no specific 'hook', but he's subtly conveyed that he's targeting their organisation in particular – and is not just sending the same letter off to dozens of different organisations.

> Having carefully researched your business and its position within the market, I am writing to outline my extensive experience and successful track record as a Sales Manager. I believe I possess the skills, qualifications and vital experience necessary to make a very significant contribution to your sales operation.

Keep it brief

Don't lose sight of the fact that your opening paragraph is just an introduction – it's essential to keep it brief. Aim for a couple of sentences; if you phrase yourself carefully that should be more than sufficient to say all that you need to say. The goal of the opening paragraph is to arouse the reader's curiosity and to lead them into your central paragraphs – which we'll be covering in the next section.

The central paragraphs: maintaining the reader's interest

Having captured the reader's attention with your opening paragraph, your task now is to maintain that interest. It's time to get down to the nitty-gritty. Your central paragraphs are critical to the success of your letter.

Your goal is to persuade the reader to take a look at your CV. To achieve this you're going to have to really arouse their interest. The reader already knows what you are interested in and has started to take an interest in you. Your challenge now is to further develop that interest and to lead them towards taking a decision in your favour.

> your goal is to persuade the reader to take a look at your CV

Establish what you really have to offer

You need to focus clearly on what you have to offer the reader and why you are interested in working for them in the role you have specified. You need to include at least two or three key sales points and you must choose these carefully.

You most likely feel there are numerous reasons why they should be interested in employing you. What you need to do is list all these out on a piece of scrap paper (or on your word-processing software) and then whittle them down until you're left with two or three points that you feel really set you apart from the competition.

 case study

> I am an extremely commercially astute and highly motivated salesman. I possess excellent interpersonal and networking skills and consequently have a natural talent for PR.

Add credibility through examples

It's all very well to say that you are x, y and z, but why should the reader believe you? Most recruiters are sufficiently experienced as not to believe everything they read. In fact, we're all inundated with empty rhetoric in the media on a daily basis. If you can go beyond making a claim to actually back it up with evidence – actually give an example of a specific achievement – then you will immediately increase your credibility.

I made the point in Chapter 1 that numbers often speak louder than words. Wherever possible you should aim to qualify your statements with specific figures if you really want to maximise the impact. Try to quote precise figures, percentages and so on.

As well as outlining your actual achievements, it can be worth spelling out the benefit experienced by your employer as a result. It is not always immediately apparent what the benefit might have been and you want to make sure that your reader is in no two minds about it.

brilliant case study

> I am an extremely commercially astute and highly motivated salesman. In my current role I have delivered a substantial increase in weekly sales levels, from £45,000 to £85,000 – very nearly double. This has resulted in a major impact on the company's bottom line.
>
> Also, as a consequence of my excellent interpersonal and networking skills, I have a natural talent for PR. Recently, I organised a thoroughly successful product launch, gaining local and national press coverage – which included my featuring in the programme 'Business Lunch' on XYZ TV, providing invaluable exposure for the business.

Did you notice how Joe also turned round the beginning of the second paragraph so that it no longer starts with 'I'? You may recall the importance of avoiding I-strain from Chapter 1.

Refer the reader to your CV

Remember that your goal is to persuade the reader to take a look at your CV? Well, don't be scared of subtly suggesting it to them. Try to slip in some sort of reference to 'my enclosed CV' and a certain percentage of readers will immediately react to this suggestion by breaking off from reading your letter to examine your CV – and your CV is your number one weapon when it comes to securing an interview.

A good idea is to tie this trick in with one of the examples you are quoting in your letter. It's a much more powerful approach than simply rolling out that old cliché, 'Please find enclosed my CV.' They're not completely stupid – they will already have noticed you've enclosed your CV! What you need to do is give them a compelling reason to look at it.

brilliant case study

I am an extremely commercially astute and highly motivated salesman. As you will note from my enclosed CV, in my current role I have delivered a substantial increase in weekly sales levels, from £45,000 to £85,000 – very nearly double. This has resulted in a major impact on the company's bottom line.

Explain your motivations

Yes, you've already told them what job you're looking for in your opening paragraph. However, the reader is also going to be asking themselves questions as to your motivations. You could be looking for a new job for any one of a multitude of different reasons, some of which you are likely to be happier to disclose than others.

'More money' is of course one of the very top reasons for looking for a new job; however, it's hard to portray this positively. Instead, you should stick to more 'constructive' reasons, such as that you are looking for more responsibility, a greater challenge and so on. And you should most definitely avoid any criticism of your current employer, no matter how thinly veiled.

A change in circumstances is also a popular reason for looking for a new job. You could of course have been made redundant. However, perhaps there is a more positive reason. Maybe you've just completed your training for a new qualification. This could be an ideal opportunity for you to score another point with the reader. Whilst they will be curious as to your motivations, what they're really interested in is what you have to offer.

 **brilliant** case study

> Having just graduated with a BA (Hons.) in Marketing and Advertising, I am now looking for a challenging new position which will enable me to make the very most of this qualification.

Show that you've done your homework

If it's at all possible to do so in passing then you should definitely try to demonstrate an understanding of their particular company or organisation. Show them that you've done your homework. This often won't be possible but, just like your opening paragraph, if you can make a worthwhile comment that is specific to their organisation, then it will undoubtedly give you an advantage.

 **brilliant** case study

> Having just graduated with a BA (Hons.) in Marketing and Advertising, I am now looking for a challenging new position. Your company does of course work closely with suppliers in France and this would be an ideal opportunity for me to make the very most of my language skills; my degree course included 2 months of valuable work experience in Marseille.

Did you notice how Joe turned round that last sentence so it started with 'Your' instead of 'I'? Again, do your best to avoid I-strain when writing your letters.

Putting it all together

 **case study**

Joe's completed central section looks like this:

> I am an extremely commercially astute and highly motivated salesman. As you will note from my enclosed CV, in my current role I have delivered a substantial increase in weekly sales levels, from £45,000 to £85,000 – very nearly double. This has resulted in a major impact on the company's bottom line.
>
> Also, as a consequence of my excellent interpersonal and networking skills, I have a natural talent for PR. Recently, I organised a thoroughly successful product launch, gaining local and national press coverage – which included my featuring in the programme 'Business Lunch' on XYZ TV, providing invaluable exposure for the business.
>
> Having just graduated with a BA (Hons.) in Marketing and Advertising, I am now looking for a challenging new position. Your company does of course work closely with suppliers in France and this would be an ideal opportunity for me to make the very most of my language skills; my degree course included 2 months of valuable work experience in Marseille.

Signing off: including your 'call to action'

The key to ending your letter is to make sure you do so in a positive, upbeat manner. You're contacting the organisation out of the blue on a totally unsolicited basis, so you can't exactly demand a response from them – but you need to do everything in your power to encourage one.

If they've taken the time to read this far into your letter then you're already making excellent progress. The last thing you want to do is lose them at the end of the letter.

The final sentence

Some people will suggest something along the following lines:

If you do not have any vacancies at present I would be grateful if you would keep my details on file for future reference.

Personally, I feel this is rather lame. I feel you should end your letter with a statement that shows a little more confidence in yourself. An employer will make their own decision as to whether to keep your details on file for future reference, regardless of whether or not you ask them to – so there's no point in asking them to do so. It just takes up valuable space in your letter and dilutes the overall impact of your message.

In any case, you don't really want them to file your details, do you? You want them to get in touch with you as soon as possible. And this is where a little advertising device known as a 'call to action' comes in handy.

Call to action

 brilliant definition

'Call to action'

This is a term used in advertising to describe a message to the reader of an advert or other promotional material that is specifically designed to motivate them to take some specific action, perhaps to pick up the phone and place an order – for example, 'Call now while stocks last!'

In the context of your cover letter, your call to action should be designed to prompt the recruiter to want to get in contact with you and, clearly, invite you for an interview.

It may seem obvious to you that if they are interested in interviewing you, all they need to do is pick up the phone, and you might feel there is not much point in stating the obvious. However, market research has clearly demonstrated that including a call to action at the end of a promotional message (which is what your letter is) increases the response rate by a statistically significant percentage.

subtly guide the reader to take the action you want them to take

So you need to subtly guide the reader to take the action you want them to take. Adopt a confident tone but try to avoid coming across as pushy. And never suggest that you will call them to follow up on your application. You might see this as enthusiasm; the recruiter will most likely see it as harassment! Put yourself in their shoes. Somebody you've never heard of writes to you looking for a job and then says they'll call you in a few days' time to arrange a meeting. It's a little too presumptive, isn't it? Some candidates even go so far as to suggest an actual date and time to meet – but 'Would tomorrow morning suit you?' is going to come across as desperate more than anything else. If they're interested then they'll contact you – you can't force it on them.

There are only so many different ways you can write this final sentence whilst abiding by all the rules.

brilliant case study

Joe chooses to close his letter with:

> Please do not hesitate to call me on 07700 900 159 so we can arrange an interview to discuss my application in greater depth.

With this one sentence, Joe has managed to:

● place the idea in the head of the reader that they may wish to interview this candidate;

● demonstrate self-confidence in his appeal to a prospective employer;

● infuse a sense of immediacy – a sense of urgency for action to be taken;

● place his key contact phone number right at the reader's fingertips;

● portray himself in a polite, courteous and professional manner;

● avoid putting the reader under unwarranted pressure.

You will most probably wish to develop your own subtle variations on this theme depending on your own circumstances and personal preferences. But you can't go too far wrong with Joe's version.

brilliant blooper

Just for a laugh, here's a classic blooper one candidate put at the end of their letter. She might not have got the job but at least she got some fame – because this quote frequently appears in lists of top cover letter gaffs:

▶

Let's meet up very soon, so you can ooh and aah over my experience!

Yes, it shows enthusiasm. Yes, it shows a lively, extrovert personality. Yes, it possibly shows she has a sense of humour.

But it's hardly very professional!

'I look forward to hearing from you'

I've talked in detail above about your 'final' sentence. However, there is one more sentence you might choose to include in your letter:

I look forward to hearing from you.

It's a standard phrase we're all familiar with and opinion is divided as to whether or not to include such a sentence. Some feel it to be tired and clichéd; others feel it to be a traditional and friendly gesture to the reader.

An alternative is:

I look forward to hearing from you and thank you for your time.

It's very much a matter of personal taste whether or not you include such a statement – and personally I think it can be quite a nice touch. It all depends on the circumstances.

 case study

Here's an example of one of Joe's completed speculative letters:

JOE BLOGGS

1 Anyold Road, Guildford AN1 1CV
Telephone: 01632 960 314 (Home); 07700 900 159 (Mobile)
Email: joebloggs@example.com

Mr. David Brennan
Sales Director
Food Distributors Limited
2 Someother Road
GUILDFORD   AN2 2CV

10 June 2009

Dear Mr. Brennan,

SALES MANAGEMENT VACANCIES

Having recently seen the article in *The Grocer* mentioning the impressive new warehousing facility you are constructing in Guildford, I am writing to outline my extensive experience and successful track record as a Sales Manager. I believe I possess the skills, qualifications and vital experience necessary to make a very significant contribution to your sales operation.

I am an extremely commercially astute and highly motivated salesman. As you will note from my enclosed CV, in my current role I have delivered a substantial increase in weekly sales levels, from £45,000 to £85,000 – very nearly double. This has resulted in a major impact on the company's bottom line.

Also, as a consequence of my excellent interpersonal and networking skills, I have a natural talent for PR. Recently, I organised a thoroughly successful product launch, gaining local and national press coverage – which included my featuring in the programme 'Business Lunch' on XYZ TV, providing invaluable exposure for the business.

Having just graduated with a BA (Hons.) in Marketing and Advertising, I am now looking for a challenging new position. Your company does of course work closely with suppliers in France and this would be an ideal opportunity for me to make the very most of my language skills; my degree course included 2 months of valuable work experience in Marseille.

Please do not hesitate to call me on 07700 900 159 so we can arrange an interview to discuss my application in greater depth.

Yours sincerely,

Joe Bloggs

enc.:   CV

Summary

- Your opening paragraph must answer four questions – why you want to work for them, what you're looking for, what you're offering and why they should care.

- Your goal in your central paragraphs is to persuade the reader to take a look at your CV. To achieve this, you're going to have to really arouse their interest.

- You need to focus clearly on what you have to offer the reader and why you are interested in working for them in the role you have specified.

- The key to ending your letter is to make sure you do so in a positive, upbeat manner. Don't demand a response but do everything in your power to encourage one.

- You need to subtly guide the reader to take the action you want them to take. Adopt a confident tone but try to avoid coming across as pushy.

Free templates

The examples in the following pages should help to illustrate all the points I have made in this chapter – and should also help you to generate useful ideas for your own letters.

These examples obviously include formatting, which it might be hard for you to copy from this book – or at the very least rather time-consuming to do so. I have therefore provided a special link for you to go online and download a full set of all the cover letters used in this book. There's no charge for this. All readers of *Brilliant Cover Letters* are entitled to this entirely for free.

Simply visit the following page to quickly and easily download your free templates: **http://www.ineedacv.co.uk/lettertemplates**.

 examples

Jason Anderson

address: 1 Anyold Road, Anywhere AN6 3RE
telephone: 01632 960 603 / 07700 900 790
email: jasonanderson@example.com

Mrs. Kim Swain
Head of Human Resources
Topper Supermarkets plc
2 Another Road
ANYWHERE   AN5 4RE

10 June 2009

Dear Mrs. Swain,

SENIOR BUYING VACANCIES

Having read with interest your latest annual report and accounts, I am writing to outline the contribution I would be able to make to your organisation as a highly experienced Senior Buying Manager.

In my current role, accountable for the Beers, Ales and Cider category, I have successfully overachieved budgeted sales by 12% (£2.5 million) whilst negotiating an additional £1.2 million in business plan support.

Other achievements include delivering total group savings of £2 million within the Vegetable, Salad and Horticulture category and creating and developing a multi-national produce buying team in the UK.

Your company's rate of growth is impressive and your plans for the future are inspirational. I would welcome the opportunity to play a part in helping you to achieve your goals. I feel the time is right for me to move on to a new challenge and, with a proven track record, I am confident of delivering major cost savings and elevated sales levels – contributing directly to your bottom line.

Please do not hesitate to call me on 07700 900 790 so we can arrange an interview to discuss my application in greater depth.

Yours sincerely,

Jason Anderson

enc.: CV

GARY SINFIELD

1 Anyold Road, Anywhere AN6 3RE
Telephone: 07700 900 532
Email: garysinfield@example.com

Ms. Denise Harris
Project Manager
Acumen Construction Limited
93 Another Road
ANYWHERE   AN5 4RE

10 June 2009

Dear Ms. Harris,

SITE MANAGEMENT VACANCIES

Having read the piece in *Building* magazine which detailed the major new housing contract you have just secured, I am writing to outline my experience as a Site Manager. I believe I possess the skills, qualifications and vital experience necessary to ensure the successful and profitable completion of this important new contract.

As you will see from my enclosed CV, in my current role I have had full responsibility for the end-to-end management of a variety of high value projects such as the recent new build of four luxury houses with a resale value of £8 million. As well as my general responsibility for all site personnel, I was also tasked with controlling costs, contributing directly to the completion of the project with a 14% cost saving. This clearly added significantly to the profit margin on resale.

Now nearing the completion of my NHBC NVQ in Site Manager Development Level IV, I am keen to further broaden my experience with a suitably challenging new project. Your company has an excellent reputation for the quality of your work and, whilst keeping costs in check is clearly vital, I have demonstrated that, with careful management, this need not be at the expense of quality standards.

Please do not hesitate to call me on 07700 900 532 so we can arrange an interview to discuss my application in greater depth.

Yours sincerely,

Gary Sinfield

enc.: CV

Gareth Hobson

1 Anyold Road, Anywhere AN6 3RE
Telephone: 07700 900 196
Email: garethhobson@example.com

Miss Esta Morris
HR Manager
Computers R Us plc
78 Another Road
ANYWHERE   **AN5 4RE**

10 June 2009

Dear Miss Morris,

SYSTEM IMPLEMENTATION VACANCIES

Having visited your stand at the IT 2009 trade fair, I am writing to detail how my expertise in system implementation could help to streamline your operations, leading to reductions in costs and increases in client satisfaction.

My main area of expertise over the past seven years has been the implementation of ERP and SCM systems. Extensive training in M3 (Movex) and JDA (Manugistics) enables me to tailor modules according to specific client requirements and to facilitate the completion of projects in accordance with challenging objectives.

I have a strong academic background and, as you will note from my enclosed CV, I am currently studying towards a Project Management professional qualification to further enhance my knowledge and understanding of the processes, systems and methodologies required for successful project implementation.

Your company currently serves an impressive array of high profile clients and I would relish the challenge of assisting you in improving your service standards whilst also realising efficiency savings. My additional experience in business analysis, consultancy and materials management is clearly also valuable in enhancing the customer experience.

Please do not hesitate to call me on 07700 900 196 so we can arrange an interview to discuss my application in greater depth.

Yours sincerely,

Gareth Hobson

enc.: CV

Ricky Woolf

1 Anyold Road, Anywhere AN6 3RE
Telephone: 07700 900 532
Email: rickywoolf@example.com

Mr. Gareth Hobson
IT Director
Corporate Giant plc
38 Another Road
ANYWHERE   AN5 4RE

10 June 2009

Dear Mr. Hobson,

NETWORK SUPPORT VACANCIES

I recently attended the graduate recruitment fair at Earls Court and spent some time discussing your organisation with your colleagues. I am consequently writing to outline the academic background and experience which would make me a valuable addition to your network support team.

As you will note from my enclosed CV, I have just graduated with an MSc in Computer Networks from Durham University, having previously achieved a first class HND in Computer Science and Engineering – where I was amongst the top three students in the whole college.

I have complemented my formal studies by gaining valuable hands-on industry experience as a Junior Network Support Engineer for Crucia Technology. I am involved in installing and maintaining LAN and cable networks and in the provision of hardware and application support.

Having completed my MSc I am now looking for a challenging position in network support and engineering where I can make the very most of my strong academic background and practical experience and contribute to the smooth and efficient operation of your IT infrastructure.

Please do not hesitate to call me on 07700 900 532 so we can arrange an interview to discuss my application in greater depth.

Yours sincerely,

Ricky Woolf

enc.:   CV

Brian McGee
1 Anyold Road, Anywhere AN6 3RE
Telephone: 07700 900 595
Email: brianmcgee@example.com

Ms. Susan Farrer
Human Resources Director
Skills Booster Limited
68 Another Road
ANYWHERE   AN5 4RE

10 June 2009

Dear Ms. Farrer,

BUSINESS DEVELOPMENT VACANCIES

Having met your Marketing Director, Wolfgang Heikel, at the recent conference in Leeds, I am writing to outline my track record in business development. I believe my experience and knowledge of the sector would be extremely useful to you in further building your market share.

I am a dedicated and driven Business Development Manager; in my current role I have been successful in delivering new business worth in excess of £480K within the space of just 12 months. As you will note from my enclosed CV, I act as an expert on NVQ and other formal qualification types, playing a pivotal role in helping the company to reach – and surpass – its defined revenue objectives.

Your company is clearly well placed to take advantage of my advanced knowledge of coaching and training in conjunction with my ability to drive a business forward. I am adept at analysing market intelligence and identifying profitable new business opportunities, leading to increased sales and, most importantly, increased profits. Having achieved my goals in my current role, I am now looking for a new challenge.

Please do not hesitate to call me on 07700 900 595 so we can arrange an interview to discuss my application in greater depth.

I look forward to hearing from you.

Yours sincerely,

Brian McGee

enc.: CV
cc: Wolfgang Heikel, Marketing Director

Janet Dunne

1 Anyold Road, Anywhere AN6 3RE
Telephone: 01632 960 511; Mobile: 07700 900 951; Fax: 01632 960 613
Email: janetdunne@example.com

Mr. Brian McGee
Senior Partner
McGee, Rumpole and Edwards Solicitors
15 Another Road
ANYWHERE   AN5 4RE

10 June 2009

Dear Mr. McGee,

TRAINEE SOLICITOR VACANCIES

As an evidently successful local legal practice, I am writing to you to outline my background and experience. I believe I possess the academic qualifications and practical experience necessary for me to be of great use to your practice as a Trainee Solicitor.

As you can see from my CV, I am currently awaiting the results of my LLM Business and Commercial Law Degree (John Moore's University), having previously achieved LLB Honours in Law.

My academic studies have been financially supported by administrative and clerical work in various legal practices and I have had the opportunity to observe and work alongside experienced fee earners, partners and counsel – which has helped to confirm my passion for this line of work.

Eager to develop my legal career further, I am looking for a new and suitably challenging position and feel I would prove a beneficial addition to your team and provide an excellent point of contact for your clients and associates. I possess outstanding interpersonal skills and enjoy building and maintaining long-term client relationships.

Please do not hesitate to call me on 07700 900 951 so we can arrange an interview to discuss my application in greater depth.

I look forward to hearing from you and thank you for your time.

Yours sincerely,

Janet Dunne

enc.:   CV

Donald Griffin
1 Anyold Road, Anywhere AN6 3RE
Telephone: 01632 960 269 (Home); 07700 900 338 (Mobile)
Email: donaldgriffin@example.com

Ms. Janet Dunne
Managing Director
Secret Squirrel Limited
45 Another Road
ANYWHERE   AN5 4RE

10 June 2009

Dear Ms. Dunne,

SECURITY VACANCIES

Being aware of the reputation your operation has established within the sector, I am writing to outline my surveillance and reconnaissance experience gained whilst serving in the British Army. I believe my abilities will be of significant value to the further development of your team.

During my army career, I specialised in the use of optics and recording equipment, ultimately responsible for a team of ten personnel undertaking covert and mobile surveillance. Whilst the precise details of our operations are classified, you will note from my CV that I am familiar with a very broad range of equipment and techniques. As a matter of national security, my training was taken very seriously indeed.

Following the completion of my military career, I am now keen to apply my skills and experience to a new challenge. I am a highly dedicated and strongly driven individual, capable of rapidly adapting to new situations.

Your organisation does of course operate within the private sector. However, I am sure you will appreciate the value of my military experience, including my ability to lead, train, motivate and supervise a highly effective team.

Please do not hesitate to call me on 07700 900 338 so we can arrange an interview to discuss my application in greater depth.

Yours sincerely,

Donald Griffin

enc.:   CV

Sarah Stevens

1 Anyold Road, Anywhere, AN6 3RE
Telephone: 01632 960 552 (Home); 07700 900 481 (Mobile)
Email: sarahstevens@example.com

Mr. Donald Griffin
Head of HR
Royal Hampshire Hospital
Scalpel Road
ANYWHERE   AN5 4RE

10 June 2009

Dear Mr. Griffin,

STAFF NURSE VACANCIES

Having recently seen on television that you will soon be opening your new paediatric ward, I am writing to outline my experience as a Staff Nurse. I believe my strong practical skills in patient care would make an important contribution to the successful operation of the new ward.

As you will see from my enclosed CV, following completion of my Diploma in Adult Nursing I have undertaken a broad range of additional professional training such as Vac-KCI Wound Management, ALERT and Immediate Life Support. I have also had the opportunity to put my skills into practice on a daily basis in my current role.

I am committed to pursuing a career path in paediatric nursing and feel sure that my unique set of skills will be a useful addition to your team. Adept at assessing patient care needs, I take pride in developing, implementing and evaluating highly effective care programmes.

Please do not hesitate to call me on 07700 900 481 so we can arrange an interview to discuss my application in greater depth.

I look forward to hearing from you and thank you for your time.

Yours sincerely,

Sarah Stevens

enc.:   CV

James Catterall
1 Anyold Road, Anywhere AN6 3RE
Telephone: 07700 900 175
Email: jamescatterall@example.com

Mrs. Sarah Stevens
Operations Director
Mugs and Cups Limited
62 Another Road
ANYWHERE　　AN5 4RE

10 June 2009

Dear Mrs. Stevens,

PROJECT MANAGEMENT VACANCIES

Having carefully researched your business and its position in the market, I am writing to outline my abilities as a Project Manager and the ways in which my experience would enable me to make a major contribution to the further success of your operations.

As you will see from my enclosed CV, I have recently been responsible for a major initiative for Welshman Crockery Systems, coordinating the critical JULIUS project following the company's win of a £20 million contract with Knives and Forks plc. I oversaw the development and implementation of sales processes and IT systems for the global production of dispenser units for use within 80 different countries.

Working to strict deadlines and tight budgets, I carefully managed all risks and resources so as to meet our goals. I also acted as a focal point of contact for the client, ensuring that their needs were fully accommodated.

Following the successful completion of this project, I am now looking for a new, challenging project management position and am certain that my combination of skills, knowledge and experience will add immediate value to your company.

Please do not hesitate to call me on 07700 900 175 so we can arrange an interview to discuss my application in greater depth.

Yours sincerely,

SUSAN FARRER

1 Anyold Road, Anywhere AN6 3RE
Telephone: 01632 960 748 (Home); 07700 900 627 (Mobile)
Email: susanfarrer@example.com

Mr. John Bycroft
Sales and Marketing Director
Novelty Products Limited
22 Another Road
ANYWHERE   AN5 4RE

10 June 2009

Dear Mr. Bycroft,

MARKETING VACANCIES

Having heard that you are planning to relocate to larger premises in London I am writing to outline my background as a Marketing Manager. I believe my experience will be of interest to you and that I would be a welcome addition to your marketing department, helping you to continue your rapid expansion.

I am a versatile and determined individual with considerable commercial know-how. As you will see from my enclosed CV, I have spent most of my career in marketing and business development, with specialist knowledge of the toy, gadget and novelty markets. I possess an exceptional track record in helping to build young companies as well as extensive account management experience.

I am now keen to develop my career further and am therefore looking for a suitably challenging new position. Your product range is impressive and the demand in the market is clear; the key is to identify new channels to market and to exploit them as effectively as possible. I am sure this is something to which I will be able to make a valuable contribution.

Please do not hesitate to call me on 07700 900 627 so we can arrange an interview to discuss my application in greater depth.

Yours sincerely,

Susan Farrer

enc.:   CV

CHAPTER 3

Advert-response letters: getting together a winning strategy

Basic principles

brilliant definition

'Advert-response letter'

An advert-response letter differs from a speculative letter in that you have already identified that the prospective employer has a specific vacancy that they are keen to fill.

In many ways, whilst generally longer than a speculative letter, an advert-response letter is easier to write – because the employer will have already given you a number of clues as to what they are looking for. They are already telling you what it is that they need.

However, much effort is still required, as you will most likely be up against a lot more competition than you would be for a speculative application. But it's not a shot in the dark – get it right and you're in with a very strong chance of winning an interview.

Choosing your targets

I'll be talking about how to actually find your targets in Chapter 9, page 189: Job hunting. The point I'd like to make in this chapter is that it's vital to choose your targets carefully. You'll need to be very selective.

Do make sure you match any criteria listed as essential to the role. There is really very little point applying for a job if you simply do not have the

> make sure you match any criteria listed as essential to the role

required qualifications and experience – it's a waste of your own time and the employer's time. You can be absolutely sure that there will be applicants who do fully meet the criteria and you clearly can't compete with them.

However, having said that, if you only just fall short of the criteria but do feel you have other qualities that will give you an edge, it may still be worth a crack. It is very much a matter of judgement whether or not you should proceed with your application. However, if you do proceed then it would be advisable to word your cover letter so as to tackle your 'weak point' and emphasise why you feel that you should still be considered for the position. (We'll cover this later in the chapter.)

First steps: read – and re-read – the advert

Undoubtedly, the key to a perfect advert-response letter – one that will really get you noticed – is the employer's advertisement itself.

The average job advert will normally contain a lot of very useful information about:

● the role itself – the specific duties and responsibilities entailed;

● the type of candidate the employer is looking for – in terms of qualifications and experience.

You need to read through this very carefully, dissect and break it down until you're left with the material you need to help you write your letter.

brilliant tip

The secret is to understand precisely what it is that the recruiter wants and then make sure that your letter (and your CV, for that matter) delivers this.

Use the job advert to help you identify exactly what it is that the prospective employer is looking for. Then, make sure you clearly demonstrate how your skills and experience not only match their requirements, but also make you the perfect candidate for the role.

If you are to be able to convince a recruiter that you are right for the role, you obviously need first to get it clear in your own mind why you are right for the role – and you can't do this unless you have properly researched and understood what it will involve.

Researching the organisation

You can even go beyond this and take a closer look at the organisation itself. What sort of organisation are they? What do they do? What is their ethos? What sort of culture do they have? What type of people do they employ?

A recruiter will expect you to have done your homework, and a lack of knowledge of the organisation will betray a lack of effort on your part. How can they be sure you really want this job – and that you're really the right candidate for it – if you know so little about their organisation?

brilliant blooper

One candidate, famously, upon being asked at interview what they could bring to the company, responded with, 'What is it that you do again?'

Try to find out as much as you can about your prospective employer. The more information you have at your fingertips the better.

The Internet is normally an excellent research tool. Most organisations will have websites where you can read all about their background, their structure and their products/services. Some will even list biographical details of key employees, maintain archives of press releases, provide downloadable financial accounts and so on. In the space of half an hour you should be able to brief yourself thoroughly.

Besides researching the organisation itself, you should try to understand the environment in which it operates. Again, the Internet is a valuable resource. However, specialist trade journals can also yield a wealth of useful information and may help you to answer the following questions:

● What industry or sector does the organisation operate within?

- How is this industry or sector currently evolving?
- Who are the main players within the industry or sector?

brilliant statistic

Approximately 80 per cent of candidates will have conducted no research whatsoever.

It's pretty obvious that if you can put yourself into the top 20 per cent of candidates who have taken the time to conduct some research, this will give you an immediate advantage.

Questions to ask yourself

For your own benefit, you will also want answers to the following kinds of question:

- What does this organisation have to offer me?
- Are they the right employer for me?
- Will there be sufficient opportunities for career progression?

brilliant case study

Joe Bloggs has seen the following job advert in one of his local newspapers:

Having recently undergone an impressive tactical acquisition, we are now one of the UK's most respected and prestigious beverage suppliers and distributors.

To help continue our expansion, we are seeking an experienced Senior Sales Manager.

You will be responsible for effecting sales campaigns, generating new business and managing and expanding existing buyer relationships.

With a minimum of five years' experience and a proven track record of business development, you will be able to demonstrate outstanding communication, organisation and negotiation skills.

A high standard of written and spoken French is desirable but not essential.

Excellent remuneration package for the right candidate. Please write with CV and details of current earnings.

This is a very typical advert. It certainly contains a lot of useful information but doesn't go into too much detail. Some adverts will be a lot more precise and really make life easy for you. Others will be much more vague – especially adverts in more prestigious newspapers and magazines where each extra word adds to the advertiser's bill.

In the rest of the chapter, we'll see how Joe develops a cover letter in response to this advert – one that will maximise his chances of getting an interview.

The opening paragraph: making an impact

How many other people are going to be applying for this job?

It could easily be over a hundred.

How are you going to make sure you stand out from the crowd?

your opening paragraph is vital in capturing the reader's attention

Your opening paragraph is vital in capturing the reader's attention. It'll normally be the first – and sometimes only – paragraph they read. Yes, you're applying for the job you've seen advertised – they'll figure that out pretty quickly. But why are you applying for this job? What do you have to offer?

If you fail to start building your case immediately, you risk losing the reader's interest in a matter of seconds.

What job are you applying for?

Before proceeding any further, you should clearly state the position you are applying for, along with any reference number(s) quoted in the job advert. It is very possible that the recruiter will simultaneously be seeking candidates for various different positions and so it will make their life a lot easier if they can see clearly and at a glance which vacancy it is that you are applying for.

I would suggest placing these details on a separate line and in bold text, immediately after your opening, 'Dear ...' You could also use capital letters for greater emphasis.

 **brilliant** case study

Here is how Joe starts his letter:

> Dear Mr. Hammond,
>
> **SENIOR SALES MANAGER VACANCY – REF. ABC123**

Standing out from the crowd

The classic opening paragraph tells the reader that you're writing to apply for the vacancy; it states where and when you heard of the vacancy and highlights the enclosure of your CV:

I am writing to apply for the above-mentioned vacancy as advertised in The Local Rag *on June 17th. Please find enclosed a copy of my CV for your perusal.*

Lame! Don't you think so?

How many other candidates will be starting their letters with almost exactly those same words?

Never miss out on an opportunity to grab the reader's attention and make an impact.

Whilst it might be traditional to say that you're writing to apply for the vacancy in question, you've already made that clear with the subject line of your letter. Whilst it might be traditional to say where and when you saw the advert, it's not necessary and it's a waste of space. Whilst it might be traditional to say that you're enclosing a copy of your CV, it's simply stating the obvious.

Unlike a speculative letter, you don't need to start off with a 'hook' to explain why you are particularly interested in them and their organisation (that can come later). The reason is self-evident – you've seen their advert. Mention this and immediately follow it up with a summary of what it is that you are offering and why that should be of interest to them. In most circumstances, this can be based on the sales pitch you'd use for a speculative letter – it's only a generic summary; the detail will come later.

 **case study**

> Having seen your advertisement for a Senior Sales Manager, I am writing to outline my extensive experience and successful track record in sales management. I believe I possess the skills, qualifications and vital experience necessary to make a very significant contribution to your sales operation.

In the very first paragraph Joe has made it clear he's applying for the advertised vacancy; he's summarised what he has to offer and he's highlighted why this should be of interest to the reader.

As a recruiter, given the choice between Joe's approach and the dozens of letters that start, 'I am writing to apply for . . .', which letter would you be more interested in reading?

Putting it all together

 **case study**

Joe's complete opening runs like this:

> Dear Mr. Hammond,
>
> **SENIOR SALES MANAGER VACANCY – REF. ABC123**
>
> Having seen your advertisement for a Senior Sales Manager, I am writing to outline my extensive experience and successful track record in sales management. I believe I possess the skills, qualifications and vital experience necessary to make a very significant contribution to your sales operation.

The central paragraphs: stating your case

The central paragraphs are the core of your letter. This is make-or-break time. If you can't succinctly make a case to the reader as to why you are the right person for this job then they might not even bother looking at your CV – and they certainly won't bother taking the time to interview you.

The onus is on you to convince them in a few short paragraphs that yours is an application that would be well worth their taking further.

Establish how you meet their criteria

When writing a speculative cover letter, you are working, to one degree or another, in the dark, making an educated guess as to what might be most of interest to a prospective employer.

When it comes to advert-response letters it's a very different situation. You need to demonstrate to the recruiter that you are pitching directly to them, and to them alone, by identifying and making specific mention of what it is they are looking for – based on their advertisement.

The advert in our case study states that the successful candidate will be:

... responsible for effecting sales campaigns, generating new business and managing and expanding existing buyer relationships.

You should aim to identify and repeat back to the reader the 'key words' that they have used in their job advert. But you need to be subtle about this.

It would clearly be rather silly to repeat this straight back to them virtually verbatim:

In my current role I have been responsible for effecting sales campaigns, generating new business and managing and expanding existing buyer relationships.

That's not to say that a lot of people don't fall into this trap though!

I'll accept that this is a fairly extreme example and it's unlikely that most candidates would be quite so blatant. However, I'm trying to illustrate the point that you must aim to be subtle when weaving the recruiter's key words into the overall flow of your cover letter.

 **case study**

In my current role, the sales campaigns I have devised and implemented have been successful both in developing existing buyer relationships and in generating valuable new business.

By carefully mirroring the recruiter's own use of language, you will definitely score points.

Back up your statements with examples

The advert says that they're looking for a candidate with:

... a minimum of five years' experience and a proven track record of business development ...

In Joe's case he's already managed to slip 'track record' into his first paragraph but, rather than repeating 'proven track record', he's changed it to 'successful track record'. He's also covered 'a minimum of five years' experience' in his first paragraph: 'my extensive experience' and 'vital experience'. He's achieved all this whilst most candidates would still be rambling on about, 'Please find enclosed my CV for your perusal.'

The advert goes on to say that the candidate should be:

... able to demonstrate outstanding communication, organisation and negotiation skills.

This is rather vague but is nonetheless typical of many job adverts – and is just the sort of demand you're going to be up against.

Remember that including brief but relevant examples as to how you meet your prospective employer's criteria can make a big difference to the credibility of your words. It's easy to make a claim, but the recruiter may feel it lacks substance unless you can back it up with a decent example.

Apply the same principles we discussed in Chapter 2, p. 45: The central paragraphs: maintaining the reader's interest. Provide examples of specific achievements, quantify them with precise figures where possible – and make clear what the benefits were.

How is Joe going to convincingly demonstrate his communication, organisation and negotiation skills? By providing compelling examples.

brilliant case study

I am extremely commercially astute and adept at negotiating highly profitable supply contracts. I have just won a contract worth £500K per annum and, whilst meeting all the customer's criteria, I nevertheless managed to build in a healthy 15% profit margin.

Also, as a consequence of my excellent communication skills, I have a natural talent for PR. Recently, I organised a thoroughly successful product launch, gaining local and national press coverage – which included my featuring in the programme 'Business Lunch' on XYZ TV, providing invaluable exposure for the business.

Looking at the organisation itself

Why do you want to work for this organisation in particular? Don't be shy of referring to the research that you have carried out on them. It helps to emphasise that you have fully understood the organisation and the way they operate – and that won't go unappreciated.

We talked about 'hooks' in Chapter 2, p. 41: The opening paragraph: capturing the reader's attention. The aim of your research is to help make it clear to them that you want to work for them specifically because of who they are, not just because you are applying for every single job that was in today's paper.

This will inevitably help your letter to stand out from all the other letters the recruiter will be receiving.

Too many candidates know little or nothing about the organisation to which they're applying. By demonstrating the research you have done, you underline your interest, enthusiasm and motivation. Show the reader that you know what you're talking about and it's bound to impress them.

show the reader that you know what you're talking about

 **case study**

In his next paragraph, Joe manages to demonstrate that he has researched the company. He simultaneously manages to cover a further point raised in their advert – not to mention casually slipping in mention of his degree:

> Your advert states that knowledge of the French language would be an advantage. The BA (Hons.) in Marketing and Advertising, which I have just completed, included 2 months of valuable work experience in Marseille. I consequently have a high standard of both written and spoken French. Your company does of course work closely with suppliers in France and this would be an ideal opportunity for me to make the very most of my language skills.

You will note that Joe has also repeated back to the reader the key words they used in their job advert: 'high standard' and 'written and spoken French'.

If your research fails to turn up a specific hook then an alternative approach is to make reference to their 'reputation'.

brilliant example

You obviously have an enviable reputation as leaders in the sector …

However, don't go overboard in terms of singing their praises, because you don't want to risk coming across as sycophantic. And if, for whatever reason, it's not appropriate to make reference to their reputation then you can simply mention your research without going into any specifics.

brilliant example

Having carefully researched your organisation and its position within the market …

What if you don't quite make the grade?

As I mentioned previously, you should avoid applying for jobs where you fail to match the essential criteria; however, if you only just fall short of the criteria and feel you have other qualities that will give you an edge then it may still be worth a shot.

Let's imagine that the advert for the job you're applying for stipulates that they require 'a thorough working knowledge of MS Access'.

Although you have little practical experience it its application, you have recently completed a CLAIT (Computer Literacy and Information Technology) qualification and so do have a very good theoretical knowledge. Demonstrating a strong theoretical understanding of a selection criterion, even if you have not yet had the opportunity in practice, is an allowable exception to our normal rule. This is because you are able to turn this weakness around and make a strength of it by using the opportunity to highlight this CLAIT qualification.

---

brilliant example

Whilst my current role does not involve the use of MS Access I have just completed an evening course leading to the CLAIT Level 1 qualification. I elected to study the optional unit in Database Manipulation and this has given me an excellent grounding in the use of MS Access which I am now keen to apply in the workplace.

To give you another example, the job advert might state that the employer is looking for someone with a minimum of five years' experience and you only have four – but you have an additional and relevant qualification that is not mentioned in the advert.

Generally speaking, though, unless you have a 'hidden ace' up your sleeve in terms of your qualifications and experience, you should avoid applying for jobs where you don't comfortably match their criteria.

Highlighting your CV

Whereas most candidates will have wasted space right at the beginning of their letter by saying, 'Please find enclosed my CV ...', you have chosen to avoid this cliché. However, you still need to encourage the reader to look at your CV. To achieve this, you can use the same technique I described for speculative letters. Take one of your key sales points and simply insert a reference to 'my enclosed CV'.

 case study

> In my current role, the sales campaigns I have devised and implemented have been successful both in developing existing buyer relationships and in generating valuable new business. As you will note from my enclosed CV, I have delivered a substantial increase in weekly sales levels, from £45,000 to £85,000 – resulting in a major impact on the company's bottom line.

How many paragraphs?

Depending on your precise circumstances, the central section of your advert-response letter could easily run to several paragraphs. Large blocks of text are hard going on the reader's tired eyes and it's therefore good practice to stick to a maximum of four or five lines per paragraph. If there's more that you need to say than will comfortably fit into five lines, either rephrase yourself or simply split it up into separate ideas and make each one of these a separate paragraph.

You should also aim to order the central paragraphs logically and more or less according to the value they contribute. Normally, the order in which issues have been raised in the advert will be a good guide, but you can vary this so as to give greater emphasis to your most powerful selling points.

Putting it all together

 case study

Joe's central section runs like this:

> In my current role, the sales campaigns I have devised and implemented have been successful both in developing existing buyer relationships and in generating valuable new business. As you will note from my enclosed CV, I have delivered a substantial increase in weekly sales levels, from £45,000 to £85,000 – resulting in a major impact on the company's bottom line.

I am extremely commercially astute and adept at negotiating highly profitable supply contracts. I have just won a contract worth £500K per annum and, whilst meeting all the customer's criteria, I nevertheless managed to build in a healthy 15% profit margin.

Also, as a consequence of my excellent communication skills, I have a natural talent for PR. Recently, I organised a thoroughly successful product launch, gaining local and national press coverage – which included my featuring in the programme 'Business Lunch' on XYZ TV, providing invaluable exposure for the business.

Your advert states that knowledge of the French language would be an advantage. The BA (Hons.) in Marketing and Advertising, which I have just completed, included 2 months of valuable work experience in Marseille. I consequently have a high standard of both written and spoken French. Your company does of course work closely with suppliers in France and this would be an ideal opportunity for me to make the very most of my language skills.

The closing paragraph: including the salary question

You've made a compelling case with your central paragraphs and you've successfully got the reader on your side. But you can't just leave them hanging there; you need to wrap up your letter with a neat – but powerful – conclusion.

> wrap up your letter with a neat – but powerful – conclusion

There are practicalities you need to address such as your availability for interview. There's also the possibility that you're going to have to deal with an employer's demands for details of your current or expected salary. This is what we'll be covering in this section – how to bring your letter to a successful close.

Availability for interview

Having, hopefully, made a powerful case for the recruiter to take your application to the next level, i.e. an interview, you need to address a basic practicality – your availability for interview.

It is always useful for a recruiter to have an upfront statement from a candidate, advising when they are – or aren't – likely to be available for interview. You should always aim to disclose this if at all possible. In some cases, the job advert will actually request this information. However, even if it doesn't, it is always a good idea to volunteer the information and plant the idea in their head – but do make sure you are available when you say you will be. If you fail to make yourself available as previously stated then it will raise questions as to how reliable and/or organised you are.

Whilst, in an ideal world, there would be no restrictions as to when you will be available, recruiters are reasonable enough to understand that you will have to work round other commitments, most notably your current job.

 **example**

> I would like to confirm that I am available for interview most afternoons. I can normally take the afternoon off, subject to a couple of days' notice.

'Please write stating current or expected salary ...'

Many job adverts will ask you for details of your current – or expected – salary, and this is often a thorny issue for a job hunter to have to deal with.

Certainly you should never volunteer this information unless you are specifically asked for it. Neither should you stick your head in the sand and pretend you didn't notice the question. If a job advert asks for your current or expected salary then you're going to have to give them an answer. Failure to do so will most likely result in your application being summarily rejected. It's not a risk worth taking.

If you've been asked to state your current salary

I would strongly recommend against any answer other than the absolute truth. It's also a good idea to emphasise that money is not your only motivator. When it comes to talking money, you never want to come across as mercenary. (The only exception to this would be for those working in money-driven and largely commission-based roles.)

brilliant case study

The advert for the job for which Joe is applying asks him to disclose 'details of current earnings'. Joe deals with this as follows:

> As requested, I currently have a basic salary of £32,200 with a Ford Mondeo company car. I also receive an annual bonus; this year it was £2,500. Whilst my remuneration is clearly important, it's most certainly not the only deciding factor in my choice of a new job and a new employer. Continuing my professional development within a suitably challenging role is also very important to me.

If you've been asked to state your expected salary

This is not nearly so simple to answer. You need to have thought through very carefully in your own mind both what salary package you can reasonably expect and what the minimum is that you would be prepared to accept. These are issues only you can decide, but it will certainly help to have an awareness of what your 'market value' really is. This will take a little research. But that's not to say you should give a precise answer. It's best to dodge the question slightly and quote a range of possibilities.

 brilliant example

The opportunities I'm currently pursuing generally involve salary packages between £35K and £40K and I am comfortable with this range. Whilst the salary on offer won't necessarily be the deciding factor in my choice, I am naturally keen to achieve a position which offers nearer the high end of this scale – a package which best reflects my worth.

The finishing touches

To end your letter you can follow exactly the same advice I gave in Chapter 2, page 49: Signing off: including your 'call to action'. An advert-response letter is no different in this respect. You need to do everything you can to encourage a response. You need to 'close' the sale.

 brilliant case study

Joe closes his letter with:

> Please do not hesitate to call me on 07700 900 159 so we can arrange an interview to discuss my application in greater depth. I look forward to hearing from you.
>
> Yours sincerely,
>
>
> **Joe Bloggs**
>
> enc.:   CV

 **case study**

Here's Joe's completed advert-response letter:

JOE BLOGGS

1 Anyold Road, Guildford AN1 1CV
Telephone: 01632 960 314 (Home); 07700 900 159 (Mobile)
Email: joebloggs@example.com

Mr. John Hammond
Sales Director
Boozy Direct Limited
Davidson Way
GUILDFORD   AN7 7CV

10 June 2009

Dear Mr. Hammond,

SENIOR SALES MANAGER VACANCY – REF. ABC123

Having seen your advertisement for a Senior Sales Manager, I am writing to outline my extensive experience and successful track record in sales management. I believe I possess the skills, qualifications and vital experience necessary to make a very significant contribution to your sales operation.

In my current role, the sales campaigns I have devised and implemented have been successful both in developing existing buyer relationships and in generating valuable new business. As you will note from my enclosed CV, I have delivered a substantial increase in weekly sales levels, from £45,000 to £85,000 – resulting in a major impact on the company's bottom line.

I am extremely commercially astute and adept at negotiating highly profitable supply contracts. I have just won a contract worth £500K per annum and, whilst meeting all the customer's criteria, I nevertheless managed to build in a healthy 15% profit margin.

Also, as a consequence of my excellent communication skills, I have a natural talent for PR. Recently, I organised a thoroughly successful product launch, gaining local and national press coverage – which included my featuring in the programme 'Business Lunch' on XYZ TV, providing invaluable exposure for the business.

Your advert states that knowledge of the French language would be an advantage. The BA (Hons.) in Marketing and Advertising, which I have just completed, included 2 months of valuable work experience in Marseille. I consequently have a high standard of both written and spoken French. Your company does of course work closely with suppliers in France and this would be an ideal opportunity for me to make the very most of my language skills.

As requested, I currently have a basic salary of £32,200 with a Ford Mondeo company car. I also receive an annual bonus; this year it was £2,500. Whilst my remuneration is clearly important, it's most certainly not the only deciding factor in my choice of a new job and a new employer. Continuing my professional development within a suitably challenging role is also very important to me.

I would like to confirm that I am available for interview most afternoons. I can normally take the afternoon off, subject to a couple of days' notice. Please do not hesitate to call me on 07700 900 159 so we can arrange an interview to discuss my application in greater depth. I look forward to hearing from you.

Yours sincerely,

Joe Bloggs

enc.:   CV

Summary

- You need to read through the employer's advertisement very carefully, dissect and break it down until you're left with the material you need to help you write your letter.

- Your opening paragraph is vital in capturing the reader's attention. It'll normally be the first – and sometimes only – paragraph they read.

- Including brief but relevant examples as to how you meet your prospective employer's criteria can make a big difference to the credibility of your words.

- Provide examples of specific achievements, quantify them with precise figures where possible – and make clear what the benefits were.

- End your letter with an appropriate call to action. You need to do everything you can to encourage a response. You need to 'close' the sale.

Free templates

The examples in the following pages should help to illustrate all the points I have made in this chapter. And don't forget that I have provided a special link for you to go online and download a full set of all the cover letters used in this book.

Simply visit the following page to quickly and easily download your free templates: **http://www.ineedacv.co.uk/lettertemplates**.

 examples

---

VICTOR WILSON

1 Anyold Road, Anywhere AN6 3RE
Telephone: 01632 960 989 (Home); 07700 900 592 (Mobile)
Email: victorwilson@example.com

Mr. Robbie Hands
Chief Executive
The Housing Company Limited
Roof Road
ANYWHERE AN4 1XM

10 June 2009

Dear Mr. Hands,

ACCOMMODATION MANAGER VACANCY – REF. 834UJK

Having seen your advert for an Accommodation Manager, I am writing to outline my background in the housing sector. I believe my experience will be of interest to you and that I would be a welcome addition to your team.

In my current role, I have responsibility for a budget of £500,000 and have successfully implemented controls to mitigate any risk of overspending. Financially astute, I possess an excellent track record of maximising profits and facilitating business expansion whilst remaining focused on the delivery of exceptional housing services.

Most of my experience lies in the strategic management of accommodation for students and keyworkers. I am of course aware that this is also the area in which you are principally active and I feel I could make a significant contribution to your operation in this respect. I have achieved optimum occupancy levels as a direct result of marketing and networking activities and have been involved in business development through tendering bids for new projects.

Your advert states that formal qualifications in the sector, whilst not essential, would be desirable. I am committed to my continuing professional development and, as you will note from my enclosed CV, have recently completed an HND in Property & Construction having previously achieved a Higher Certificate in Managing Student Accommodation and an HNC in Housing Studies. I am also a Practitioner Member of the Institute of Housing.

I would like to confirm that I am available for interview at short notice. Please do not hesitate to call me on 07700 900 592 so we can arrange an interview to discuss my application in greater depth. I look forward to hearing from you.

Yours sincerely,

Victor Wilson

enc.: CV

James Clark

address: 1 Anyold Road, Anywhere AN6 3RE
telephone: 01632 960 623
mobile: 07700 900 487
email: jamesclark@example.com

Mrs. Joan McIntyre
Managing Director
Technical Stuff Limited
Horris Hill Business Park
ANYWHERE   AN9 9DD

10 June 2009

Dear Mrs. McIntyre,

ELECTRICAL ENGINEER VACANCY – REF. MOZ947

Having seen your advertisement for an Electrical Engineer, I am writing to outline the academic background and experience which would make me a valuable addition to your team.

With a BSc (Hons.) in Electrical and Electronic Engineering I possess extensive technical acumen and, as you will note from my CV, considerable field-based experience. I have a proven ability in providing expert advice and guidance to customers whilst delivering installation, repair and maintenance projects to strict deadlines and budgetary constraints. I possess strong faultfinding and diagnostic skills, a keen eye for detail and am committed to delivering the highest standards of customer service.

I now wish to develop my career further and am therefore looking for a new and suitably challenging position. I am aware that you have recently relocated to larger premises and am keen to make a major contribution to a successful and growing company.

With regard to your request for my expected salary, the opportunities I'm currently pursuing generally involve salary packages between £25K and £30K and I am comfortable with this range. Whilst the salary on offer won't necessarily be the deciding factor in my choice, I am naturally keen to achieve a position which offers nearer the high end of this scale – a package which best reflects my worth.

I would like to confirm that I am available for interview most days; I can normally take time off work at fairly short notice. Please do not hesitate to call me on 07700 900 487 so we can arrange an interview to discuss my application in greater depth.

Yours sincerely,

James Clark

enc.:   CV

JAYNE BERESFORD

1 Anyold Road, Anywhere AN6 3RE
Telephone: 01632 960 343 (Home); 07700 900 584 (Mobile)
Email: jaynebere sford@example.com

Mrs. Kelly Smith
Headteacher
Somenice School
Academic Lane
ANYWHERE AN6 7TY

10 June 2009

Dear Mrs. Smith,

EXAMINATIONS OFFICER VACANCY – REF. 493DIH

Having seen your advertisement for an Examinations Officer, I am writing to outline my background and experience and the ways in which my skills and abilities make me ideally suited to this role.

As you will see from my CV, I have enjoyed a diverse and rewarding career. Whilst for most of the last ten years I have worked within administration, I have just spent an extremely rewarding year as a Learning Mentor on a part-time basis at The Smart School.

Dealing with children on a one-to-one basis and in group sessions, I encouraged them to overcome any barriers to learning which could arise from issues relating to particular staff members or personal problems with confidence and self-esteem. I enjoyed considerable success in this capacity, helping my students to achieve better grades by enabling them to re-engage in learning.

I now wish to further develop my career within the education sector and am keen to take on this crucial role as an Examinations Officer. I thrive on helping children to achieve their very best. I possess excellent communication, organisation and time management skills and fully appreciate that there's no margin for error when it comes to exams.

I would like to confirm that I am available for interview at short notice. Please do not hesitate to call me on 07700 900 584 so we can arrange an interview to discuss my application in greater depth. I look forward to hearing from you.

Yours sincerely,

Jayne Beresford

enc.:   CV

NEIL KELLY

1 Anyold Road, Anywhere AN6 3RE
Telephone: 01632 960 325 (Home); 07700 900 865 (Mobile)
Email: neilkelly@example.com

Mr. James Clark
Human Resources Director
Centrenico Limited
Horris Hill Business Park
ANYWHERE   AN9 9DD

10 June 2009

Dear Mr. Clark,

TECHNICAL SUPPORT ENGINEER VACANCY – REF. 805CRW

Having seen your advertisement for a Technical Support Engineer, I am writing to outline my significant experience in this realm. I believe I possess the skills, qualifications and vital experience necessary to make a major contribution to your operations.

My career to date has focussed on the provision of effective 1st and 2nd line IT support in demanding private and public sector environments. As you will see from my enclosed CV, this practical experience is underpinned by a sound academic background in Computer Science, culminating in my MCSE qualification.

Adept at analysing and documenting project scope and progress, I have demonstrated the ability to oversee the delivery of a wide range of mission critical projects. Your company has an impressive client base, consisting of both private and public sector organisations, and I feel that my background renders me an ideal candidate for this role.

I would like to confirm that I am available for interview all day every Monday but, if it facilitates matters for you, I can normally take some time off work most days – subject to a couple of days' notice.

Please do not hesitate to call me on 07700 900 865 so we can arrange an interview to discuss my application in greater depth. I look forward to hearing from you.

Yours sincerely,

Neil Kelly

enc.:   CV

ROBBIE HANDS

1 Anyold Road, Anywhere AN6 3RE
Telephone: 01632 960 609 (Home); 07700 900 142 (Mobile)
Email: robbiehands@example.com

Mr. Neil Kelly
Senior Partner
Kelly, Thomson and Tompkins Solicitors
Judge Drive
ANYWHERE   AN6 7HS

10 June 2009

Dear Mr. Kelly,

SOLICITOR VACANCY

Having seen your advert for a Solicitor, I am writing to outline my academic qualifications and practical experience which I feel would make me of great use to your practice in this role.

As you will see from my enclosed CV, I am a highly motivated, resourceful and hard-working legal professional with significant legal and public sector experience, in addition to a recent postgraduate qualification in International Law and World Economy.

I possess an exceptional degree of integrity, judgement and tact in handling sensitive and confidential material, and am adept at working in multicultural environments, building and maintaining strong working relationships. Focused and diligent, I enjoy responsibility and can effectively prioritise and manage demanding workloads in order to meet specific objectives.

I now wish to further develop my career and, since yours is evidently a very successful local legal practice, the advertised position is of significant interest to me.

As requested, my salary is currently £37,500. Whilst my remuneration is clearly important, it's most certainly not the only deciding factor in my choice of a new job and a new employer. Continuing my professional development within a suitably challenging role is also very important to me.

I would like to confirm that I am available for interview most days, subject to a couple of days' notice. Please do not hesitate to call me on 07700 900 142 to arrange an interview.

Yours sincerely,

Robbie Hands

enc.:   CV

DENISE HARRIS

1 Anyold Road, Anywhere AN6 3RE
Telephone: 01632 960 227 (Home); 07700 900 287 (Mobile)
Email: deniseharris@example.com

Ms. Julie Humphries
Office Manager
Fast Films Limited
Alfred Avenue
ANYWHERE   AN2 4LC

10 June 2009

Dear Ms. Humphries,

PERSONAL ASSISTANT TO THE ART DIRECTOR – REF. A1FB23

Having seen your advertisement for a Personal Assistant, I am writing to outline the contribution I would be able to make to your company as a highly experienced PA.

As you will see from my enclosed CV, I am accustomed to a demanding role with long hours and significant pressure to meet strict deadlines, taking full responsibility for my decisions and understanding the importance of full support and assistance at all times.

I believe that my key qualities are my excellent interpersonal skills and strong communicative ability, combined with my talent for effective organisation and prioritisation. I see myself as a highly dedicated and strongly driven individual.

Your advert states that knowledge of film-making and photography would be an advantage. I am a keen semi-professional photographer, specialising in boudoir style photography with an emphasis for the female client. I am familiar with the work of Fast Films and would be delighted to have the opportunity to work with you.

I would like to confirm that I am available for interview most days, subject to a couple of days' notice. Please do not hesitate to call me on 07700 900 287 so we can arrange an interview to discuss my application in greater depth.

I look forward to hearing from you and thank you for your time.

Yours sincerely,

Denise Harris

enc.:   CV

DR SAMANTHA BRYAN

1 Anyold Road, Anywhere AN6 3RE
Telephone: 01632 960 967
Mobile: 07700 900 173
Fax: 01632 960 565
Email: samanthabryan@example.com

Mr. Victor Wilson
Senior Partner
The Pet Hospital
Rodent Road
ANYWHERE   AN2 6RT

10 June 2009

Dear Mr. Wilson,

PET HOSPITAL BUSINESS MANAGER VACANCY

Having seen your advert for a Business Manager, I am writing to outline my experience and the ways in which I could make a major contribution to the further success of your operations.

In my current role as a Business Development Manager I have full accountability for managing a veterinary pharmaceutical portfolio throughout the South-East and, as you will note from my enclosed CV, have been successful in increasing sales by 7%. This has been achieved as a direct result of my creating and implementing innovative marketing strategies – strategies which could be applied to increasing your client base.

In my previous role, as a Practice Manager, I was responsible for facilitating the continuous improvement of the clinic, conducting extensive research into the latest technologies and industry developments. I also provided training and support to technicians and assistants in order to improve their levels of competence and efficiency.

Your advert states that a background in veterinary medicine would be an advantage. I actually qualified as a veterinary surgeon in 2003 and am adept at performing a wide range of procedures. Whilst I have since decided that my interest lies in practice management rather than medicine, I believe that my combination of business acumen and in-depth medical knowledge makes me an ideal choice for the advertised vacancy. I am already familiar with the work you do and would relish the challenge of enhancing an already impressive reputation.

I would like to confirm that I am available for interview most days, subject to a couple of days' notice. Please do not hesitate to call me on 07700 900 173 so we can arrange an interview to discuss my application in greater depth. I look forward to hearing from you.

Yours sincerely,

Samantha Bryan

enc.:   CV

John Bycroft
1 Anyold Road, Anywhere AN6 3RE
Telephone: 01632 960 836 (Home); 07700 900 447 (Mobile)
Email: johnbycroft@example.com

Mr. David Brench
Operations Director
Big Benn & Sons Limited
Horris Hill Business Park
ANYWHERE   AN9 9DD

10 June 2009

Dear Mr. Brench,

QUALITY PRODUCT/PROCESS AUDITOR VACANCY – REF. BER105

Having seen your advert, I am writing to outline my experience as a Quality Product/Process Auditor. I believe I possess the skills, qualifications and experience necessary to successfully fulfil this vital role; I am certain that I will be able to add real value to your operation.

As you will see from my enclosed CV, I have spent the past 13 years with Julius Darkwood & Sons where I was responsible for the management of quality improvement initiatives and audit tasks, ensuring the highest possible standards were maintained on all product lines.

My duties included the implementation of specification amendments for graded ware, the completion of audits on specific materials and the review of recorded variables taken by technicians to ensure they remained in line with variable audits. I was also tasked with the completion of monthly and weekly reports on quality improvements for senior management.

As requested, my previous salary was £18,750. However, whilst salary is clearly important, I am most keen to achieve a role which will enable me to take on new challenges and broaden my experience.

I would like to confirm that I am available for interview at short notice. Please do not hesitate to call me on 07700 900 447 to arrange an interview to discuss my application in greater depth.

Yours sincerely,

John Bycroft

enc.:   CV

Rachel Brown
1 Anyold Road, Anywhere AN6 3RE
Telephone: 07700 900 926
Email: rachelbrown@example.com

Mrs. Samantha Bryan
Head of Human Resources
Princess Mary Hospital
Leeches Lane
ANYWHERE   AN3 9GV

10 June 2009

Dear Mrs. Bryan,

RISK MANAGEMENT MIDWIFE BAND 7 VACANCY – REF. AD955

Having seen your advertisement for a Risk Management Midwife, I am writing to outline my experience in this field. I believe my strong practical skills in patient care would make an important contribution to the operation of your department.

In my current role, I work as a Midwife Coordinator dealing with upwards of 3,500 deliveries per annum, including caring for high risk patients, ensuring both their well-being and that of the newborn. As you will note from my enclosed CV, I am adept at handling both premature and postmature births and all the complications that these may entail.

Your advert states that a thorough knowledge of ISO regulations would be an advantage. One of my key current responsibilities is ensuring full compliance with both policy and procedural guidelines in line with ISO regulations.

I am committed to ensuring that the highest standards of care are delivered to patients at all times and your hospital obviously has an enviable reputation for its standard of patient care.

Now wishing to further develop my career, I am looking for a suitable new challenge and feel that I would really be able to achieve results in this role.

I would like to confirm that, as a result of my shift patterns, I am available for interview all day on Monday, Tuesday and Wednesday for the month ahead. Please do not hesitate to call me on 07700 900 926 so we can arrange an interview to discuss my application in greater depth.

Yours sincerely,

Rachel Brown

enc.:   CV

Joan McIntyre

1 Anyold Road, Anywhere AN6 3RE
Telephone: 01632 960 448 (Home); 07700 900 661 (Mobile)
Email: joanmcintyre@example.com

Miss Rachel Brown
Sales Director
Big Department Store plc
High Street
ANYWHERE   AN9 9DD

10 June 2009

Dear Miss Brown,

FASHION MERCHANDISER VACANCY – REF. YO6J91

Having seen your advertisement for a Fashion Merchandiser, I am writing to detail the qualifications, skills and experience I possess which would be very beneficial for this role.

I have just graduated with a BA (Hons.) in Textile and Fashion Management and have additionally gained valuable work experience at Sascha. As you will note from my enclosed CV, I worked closely with the buying team to accurately forecast trends and plan stock levels accordingly.

Commercially astute, I fully appreciate the paramount importance of managing the performance of ranges so as to maximise profits.

I have developed considerable insight into the fashion sector and an eye for market trends and am eager to further develop my career in this direction. I have frequently visited your store and your fashion department is enviable; I would be delighted to have the opportunity to contribute to its further success.

May I confirm that I am available for interview at short notice. Please do not hesitate to call me on 07700 900 661 so we can arrange an interview to discuss my application in greater depth.

I look forward to hearing from you.

Yours sincerely,

Joan McIntyre

enc.:   CV

CHAPTER 4

Specialist cover
letters –
including letters
of application

n most lines of work, a one-page cover letter with accompanying CV is all that a prospective employer is likely to ask of you. However, there are certainly exceptions to this – and the aim of this chapter is to help prepare you to deal with those exceptions.

Some employers will of course prefer an application form system – which often doesn't involve a cover letter at all – but we'll discuss application forms in greater detail in Chapter 9.

This chapter will instead focus on the so-called 'letters of application', looking in further detail at a few popular lines of work where such letters are increasingly the norm.

Letters of application

What exactly is a letter of application?

Aren't the speculative and advert-response letters that we've already covered letters of application?

Most recruiters refer to a speculative or advert-response letter quite simply as a 'cover letter'. If you're ever specifically asked for a 'letter of application' they're normally expecting something quite different from you.

brilliant definition

'Letter of application'

A letter of application is a cross between a traditional advert-response letter and the 'personal statement' section of a traditional application form.

Letters of application are more popular in some sectors than others, but a lot depends on the whims of the individual employer. Regardless of your line of work, you might occasionally find yourself faced with a request for a letter of application, so it pays to know how to handle them.

> creating a powerful advert-response letter is the best starting point

Creating a powerful advert-response letter is the best starting point. This will give you the basic skeleton you need for a successful letter of application. However, you will be expected to build on this considerably.

Your task is to examine the job description and/or person specification in detail and demonstrate in your letter of application exactly how you meet their criteria, backing up your statements with specific examples where possible.

Isn't this what you'd do for an advert-response letter anyway?

Yes. But the difference is the level of detail you will be required to give. The end result will inevitably stretch to a couple of pages – possibly even more.

Whilst it's undoubtedly a fair amount of work, if you get it right it is also a great opportunity for you to sell yourself and really steal a march on your competition.

Teaching

One profession where letters of application are especially popular is the teaching profession.

When applying for jobs in teaching, a powerful cover letter – or letter of application – can almost be more important than the CV it accompanies.

Recruiters for teaching posts place great emphasis on the cover letter and will expect you to go into a much higher level of detail than the 'average' cover letter, particularly for the more senior vacancies.

It is a good idea to briefly summarise your academic qualifications, highlighting any that are linked to your specialist subject area. Continuing Professional Development (CPD) is of course very important in teaching – and your cover letter is a good opportunity to elaborate further on any additional training, including INSET (In-Service Education and Training) days. You can then go on to emphasise significant achievements such as positive Ofsted inspections or record exam results.

Whilst you will no doubt have covered this in your CV, it is also worth making brief mention of your involvement in extracurricular activities. Recruiters will be looking for evidence that you really want to get involved with all aspects of school life, contribute to the community and build relationships with their students both in and out of the classroom.

Of particular importance for teaching positions is the ability to demonstrate in your letter that you have researched the specific school in question and that you share their vision and ethos. The 'personal touch' is vital.

Medicine

Although recruitment to medical posts is increasingly conducted via application forms, a letter of application with accompanying CV is still essential for many vacancies.

As a medical professional, you'll possess extensive qualifications following many years of training – and very possibly many years of experience. Your prospective employers will definitely want to know all about this, and so your cover letter will inevitably be more complex – and longer – than the average.

There are a number of different areas you may want to consider highlighting in your cover letter:

- Clinical skills
- Audits

- Research
- Presentations
- Publications
- Teaching

 **brilliant** tip

You should aim to order the paragraphs of your letter logically and more or less according to the value that they contribute.

As for teachers, it is important to demonstrate CPD. Yours is a profession where you are expected to be continually learning – and much value is placed on this by employers.

Fitting all this into two pages may not be easy. However, if your letter starts to exceed two pages then you may be falling into the trap of packing in an excessive amount of information. This could make it harder for your key selling points to stand out.

try to summarise and remain concise

Try to summarise and remain concise. A prospective employer can always ask for further information if they require it – maybe at your interview.

Academia

Academic and scientific cover letters have many similarities with medical cover letters.

There will be a lot of information that you need to communicate – and that a prospective employer may be expecting you to communicate. However, you must be careful not to provide too much detail, such as overly long descriptions of projects, excessive technical detail and so on.

You might be itching to write extensive descriptions of the work you've undertaken, but it's vital to summarise and to stick to the main points. You can always elaborate at your interview if necessary. Packing too much information into your letter is likely to reduce your chances of winning an interview in the first place.

You may need to use specialist terminology to illustrate your points but, as I have previously pointed out, excessive jargon is not a good idea. If you need to use a specialist/technical term that you are not sure the reader will understand, it is perfectly acceptable to follow it with a brief definition in brackets.

Other sectors

As I mentioned earlier, you could find yourself faced with a request for a letter of application in almost any sector. They are particularly popular in teaching, medicine and academia but are also common in many other sectors. Let's look at an example for a senior role in the charity sector.

MARY DAVIES

2 Anyold Road, Guildford AN1 1CV
Telephone: 01632 960 159 (Home); 07700 900 265 (Mobile)
Email: marydavies@example.com

Mrs. Jane Jenkins
Chief Executive Officer
The Foundation
Littleold Road
GUILDFORD   AN5 3CV

10 June 2009

Dear Mrs. Jenkins,

DEVELOPMENT DIRECTOR – REF. 123ABC

Having seen your advertisement for a Development Director, I am writing to outline my unique combination of skills, capabilities and experience. I believe I will be able to add significant value to the Foundation and to the post of Development Director in particular.

As you will note from my enclosed CV, my first venture into charitable work was a project I worked on with a group of young second-generation African immigrants from deprived inner-city backgrounds. Together, we worked on the production of a film which had such a great impact that I decided to establish a registered charity, Thameside Pictures, to formally continue the project. The main aim of the charity was to provide a creative outlet for young people aged 16 – 25, the idea being to minimise instances of anti-social behaviour. We relied entirely on funding to sustain each filming project undertaken and it was during this time that I first demonstrated a natural flair for fundraising. Through networking with other charity organisations such as Awards for All, Lloyds TSB Trust and the Headley Foundation, I was able to raise funding in excess of £50K in just 12 months, enabling the production of two further film projects.

Thameside Pictures became well known within the youth, community, voluntary and statutory sectors for the positive work it carried out and, in 2006, I was approached by The Community Association to become Chair of their Board of Trustees. The charity operates a community centre providing leisure activities, training, advice and child care facilities to people from various cultural backgrounds including Morocco, Somalia, Portugal, Bosnia, Iraq and Kurdistan. I personally served on the Financial and Personnel Sub Committees involved in increasing revenues and minimising expenditure whilst also managing all staffing or disciplinary matters that arose.

The success I enjoyed with Thameside Pictures and The Community Association led to my being headhunted by the registered charity Next Generation where I currently hold the position of Operations Manager. The charity focuses on the top 5% of deprived areas in the UK and specialises in the management of community projects primarily targeting children and youths. Substantial increases in the needs of the community have resulted in the charity expanding over the last 18 months from initially just 2 members of staff to a current team of 6. In this role, I am personally responsible for the creation of all funding applications for individual project and core cost grants ranging from £2,500 to £250K. My key achievements include writing a successful partnership bid to the Primary Care Trust for £750K. I have also prepared and submitted successful bids to various other trusts, foundations and corporations. I use my strong research skills to identify funding opportunities and donors and I have established an extensive contacts network amongst grant-giving and statutory organisations.

I am familiar with the support that the Foundation has provided to Disability Action Network through its Health Award and the Education & Protection Impact Awards and, having met with a number of profoundly disabled young people over the years, I am acutely aware of the exceptional people that are required to run the projects that the Foundation supports. I also appreciate that successful funding is paramount to maintaining the level of aid required and I believe that my extensive experience will enable me to rise to the challenges associated with the role of Development Director. I am confident that I can target the most suitable corporate donors according to the Foundation's objectives and firmly believe that the valuable causes that the Foundation champions will help to ensure that the valuable funding is secured.

Alongside my charitable work, I possess a strong commercial background having spent three years managing a highly successful retail sports and urban clothing retail outlet, where I had full accountability for the management of the business from a financial, operational and administrative perspective. I developed innovative sales and marketing strategies to promote the business in a competitive sector and, through negotiations and relationship management with high profile suppliers of branded products, I was able to secure the best possible quality products at competitive prices. One of my most significant achievements during this time was in writing a comprehensive business plan which was used to secure business expansion funding of £100K from GLE.

I would be delighted to have the opportunity to discuss my application in greater depth at interview. Please do not hesitate to call me on 07700 900 265 so that we might arrange this.

I look forward to hearing from you.

Yours sincerely,

Mary Davies

enc.:   CV

CHAPTER 5

Digital considerations – email and fax

We live in an increasingly digital world and, as I mentioned in Chapter 1, I readily expect you to be making the majority of your applications by email (or fax) rather than by post.

Email and fax differ from good old-fashioned snail mail in a number of ways, and I will be discussing these differences – and how to handle them – in this chapter.

Emailing your application

email is increasingly the preferred method of sending documents

Email is increasingly the preferred method of sending documents. It is perfectly possible that you will end up making the majority of your applications by email rather than by post.

I have heard it said that 'cover letters are for the pre-Internet era' – the suggestion being that for most job applications, all you need to do is send an email with your CV attached.

But what do you say in your email?

You say exactly what you would in a 'traditional', printed cover letter.

The only real difference is the method used to send the letter. Pretty much all of the other rules of cover letter writing still apply:

- You still need to make an impact.
- You're still competing against countless others for the reader's attention.

- You still need to give them a compelling reason to read your CV (except that in this case they won't have it right there in front of them; they actually need to click to open it).

However, there are certain practicalities that you need to deal with.

Email etiquette

'Subject' line

Never leave it blank! It's extremely unprofessional to do so. But do keep it short and simple. You could specify the vacancy title and reference if applicable. If you're making a speculative application, on the other hand, you might need to be a little more inventive and make a greater effort to catch the recipient's attention. Don't go over the top though; you certainly don't want to risk your email being labelled as spam and discarded.

Form of address

You can of course remove any text from the date upwards – your letter-head and the recipient's name and address. All of this is superfluous when applying by email. The first line of your email can simply start, 'Dear ...'

start your email just as you would a printed letter

Please bear in mind that just because this is an email, that's no reason to start with 'Hi,' or suchlike. Start your email just as you would a printed letter: 'Dear ...' This isn't an email to a pal; it's an important business letter.

Content

I would definitely not recommend sending your cover letter as an email attachment. The chances of it getting read will drop dramatically. Whilst CVs should always be sent as attachments (because they normally look awful when copied and pasted into an email), you should place the contents of your cover letter in the body of your email.

Signature

Many people have an automated email 'signature' that goes out at the bottom of every email they send. Whatever yours says, remember that it will be seen by potential employers. You might decide a rewrite is in order! A good idea is to repeat your telephone number(s).

Filenames

Don't just call your CV 'CV'. Make sure it contains your name, e.g. 'Joe Bloggs – CV'. Organisations receive so many files simply called 'CV'. It's easy for confusions to arise.

File format

Microsoft Word is the most universally accepted format for a document (apart from 'plain text' – which is really not very attractive). If you send your CV in a different format, such as PDF, Mac and so on, then you're immediately reducing the chances of the recipient being able to access it (unless you work in a creative field, e.g. graphic design). Do you think the recipient will write politely back and ask for your CV in a different format? Or do you think it's more likely they'll just delete your email?

Cc and Bcc

In rare cases where your application needs to be sent to more than one individual, you might need to use the Cc function – and possibly even the Bcc function. However, it should go without saying that you shouldn't use these functions to spam multiple employers with exactly the same email. Each application you make should be tailored for the organisation to which you are sending it.

All of the example letters given in this book have been laid out on the basis that they are being sent by post. However, as you will see from the simple guidelines above, it's very easy to adapt them to email format.

Faxing your application

Fax is less and less popular these days as a means of rapid document transmission. It has been totally overtaken by email. Nevertheless, some circumstances will still require an application to be submitted by fax and I am therefore occasionally asked how to deal with this.

One young lady recently asked me, 'Should I print the cover letter on the fax cover sheet or just do a normal letter and put a fax cover sheet on it?'

↗ **brilliant** blooper

Be careful with your files and your filenames. I once received a file from a job applicant, entitled 'CV', which simply said:

what's at the bottom of my garden?

Spider
Worm
Beetle
Bug

Needless to say, he didn't get the job ...

Whereas when emailing your CV and cover letter, I would definitely not recommend sending both files as attachments, my recommendation when faxing would be to send the letter separately rather than including it on the fax cover sheet.

Unlike an email, where the recipient has to open any attachments, the recipient of a fax hasn't got much choice but to see each and every page you are sending them. This gives you the opportunity to send a properly laid-out and formatted letter, rather than trying to scrunch your message up on to a fax cover sheet.

And what should you do if you don't get a reply? Should you follow up by sending yet another fax? Or is it better (assuming you have an address) to post your follow-up? This is another popular question.

My answer is that you would actually be much better off following up by telephone. You're not harassing the recruiter; you're simply politely enquiring to see whether or not they safely received your fax. Once you've got them on the phone they're much more likely to remember you when short-listing – and this is likely to work to your advantage. You stop being a random name and start becoming a real human being.

Summary

- When sending an email, never leave your 'Subject' line blank. Specify the vacancy title and reference if applicable.

- Don't send both your CV and your cover letter as email attachments. The contents of your cover letter should be placed in the body of your email.

- Don't just call the file for your CV 'CV'. Make sure it contains your name, e.g. 'Joe Bloggs – CV'. Organisations receive so many files simply called 'CV'.

- Whatever your email signature says, remember that it will be seen by potential employers.

- When faxing, send your cover letter separately rather than including it on the fax cover sheet. Follow up by telephone rather than sending another fax.

CHAPTER 6

The 15 most common cover letter mistakes – and how to avoid them

have seen many, many thousands of letters, covering pretty much every possible kind of job and situation – and the difference in them is vast. However, the same common mistakes crop up time and time again. Too many jobseekers miss out on their dream job because of a small number of easily avoided blunders.

Some of the mistakes that people make when writing their cover letter are very obvious whilst others are much more subtle. The CV Centre has conducted a comprehensive analysis of over 1,000 cover letters to derive a 'top 15'. In this chapter I will list these 15 most common cover letter writing mistakes and refer you back to previous chapters where necessary, to explain why they are a mistake and also how to avoid them.

1 Failing to write to the right person

The best person to address your cover letter to is clearly the person who is going to be making the decision as to whether or not to interview you. Too many letters are simply addressed to the 'HR Manager' and start, 'Dear Sir/Madam'. You want to try to get right through to the decision maker. This is an elementary sales tactic but, unless you work within sales yourself, you're unlikely to be aware of how important it is to reach the person who actually has the power to make the decision you want them to make.

For further details on obtaining contact names, please refer back to Chapter 1, page 3: First things first: who are you writing to?

2 Not including your own full contact details

start all your letters with a professional-looking letterhead

I would recommend that you start all your letters with a professional-looking letterhead. It is vital that the reader can spot, at a glance, not only your name but also precisely how to get in contact with you. Put your name at the very top, followed by your key contact details – address, phone number, email address and so on. Place your address on one line, with your phone numbers on the next, and finish with your email address.

To find out exactly how to put together your own letterhead, please take a look at Chapter 1, page 5: Structure: building your skeleton letter.

3 Inappropriate email addresses

Whilst having no email address at all on your letter is clearly a problem, it's not something I see very often. Far more common is the use of fun or jokey email addresses.

Whilst these may be fine for corresponding with friends and family, employers will probably regard more 'serious' email addresses as simply more professional.

You might have taken time to put together a brilliant cover letter, but if your email address is mrluvverman@example.com then it may harm your chances. I would suggest you open a new email account to use for professional purposes (e.g. Hotmail or Yahoo!) and keep your professional correspondence separate from your personal correspondence.

To learn more about how to handle email addresses, please see Chapter 1, page 7: Structure: building your skeleton letter.

4 Losing the reader's interest with your opening words

The primary goal of your opening paragraph is, of course, to explain to the reader why it is that you are writing to them.

Your opening paragraph is vital in capturing the reader's attention. It'll normally be the first – and sometimes only – paragraph they read.

Yes, you're applying for a job – they'll figure that out pretty quickly. But why are you applying for this job? If you fail to start building your case immediately, you risk losing the reader's interest right from the very start.

The opening paragraph of your letters is discussed in both Chapter 2, page 41: The opening paragraph: capturing the reader's attention, and Chapter 3, page 71: The opening paragraph: making an impact.

5 Not saying what job you're looking for

At the beginning of your letter, you should always clearly state the position you are applying for, along with any reference number(s) quoted in the job advert. It is very possible that the recruiter will simultaneously be seeking candidates for various different positions, and so it will make their life a lot easier if they can see clearly and at a glance which vacancy it is that you are applying for.

For more information on how to craft your opening paragraph, please refer back to Chapter 2, page 41: The opening paragraph: capturing the reader's attention, and Chapter 3, page 71: The opening paragraph: making an impact.

6 Failing to make your case

Whilst it would definitely be a mistake to arrogantly oversell yourself, it is also a mistake to undersell yourself. Don't be afraid to blow your own trumpet and show a little self-confidence in what it is that you have to offer a prospective employer. It's a tight job market out there. You need to compete effectively if you're to stand any chance of achieving your career goals.

It's also important to put the right spin on your case. Always phrase yourself in terms of:

- what you have to offer the organisation;
- what you can do for the organisation;

- why it would be in their interest to hire you;

- how hiring you would add value to their organisation.

Make sure you give them compelling reasons to invite you for an interview.

If appropriate, back up your statements with real-life examples rather than just speaking hypothetically. Illustrating your points with specific, relevant examples from your own experience will dramatically increase their impact.

7 Repeating what is written in your CV

Too many people fall into the trap of repeating too much of what their CV already says. This is not only likely to weaken the impact of the letter, but may also put a recruiter off reading the CV.

Whilst you should definitely highlight certain key aspects of your CV in your cover letter, you should avoid simply copying and pasting.

A cover letter is an opportunity to draw the reader's attention to some of your key selling points – skills, experience, achievements – and to do so in a way that makes it clear how these will be of interest and potential benefit to the reader.

---

your cover letter should introduce your CV – not replace it

They've got a copy of your CV. Your cover letter should complement it – not repeat it. Your cover letter should introduce your CV – not replace it.

Nobody wants to read the same thing twice.

Nobody wants to read the same thing twice.

8 Lack of 'call to action'

The key to ending your letter is to make sure you do so in a positive, upbeat manner. You can't exactly demand a response from the reader, but you need to do everything in your power to encourage one.

This is where a little advertising device known as a 'call to action' comes in handy.

'Call to action' is a term used in advertising to describe a message to the reader of an advert or other promotional material that is specifically designed to motivate them to take some specific action, perhaps to pick up the phone and place an order – for example, 'Call now while stocks last!'

For a more detailed discussion on the topic of 'calls to action' – and how they apply to your letters – please refer back to Chapter 2, page 49: Signing off: including your 'call to action'.

9 Talking about money before you've even got your foot in the door

You should certainly never voluntarily bring up the question of money in an initial cover letter. It can be a fatal mistake, because it sends a clear message to the reader that you are more focused on your own needs than you are on theirs.

Many job adverts will, of course, specifically ask you for details of your current – or expected – salary, and you're not going to get away with pretending you didn't notice the question! If a job advert asks for your current or expected salary then you're going to have to give them an answer. Failure to do so will most likely result in your application being summarily rejected. It's not a risk worth taking.

To learn how best to handle this thorny issue, please take a look at Chapter 3, page 81: The closing paragraph: including the salary question.

10 Giving the reader I-strain

The word 'I' is often overused in cover letters. Unlike a CV, a cover letter should of course be written in the first person. However, if you start every sentence with 'I' then it can make for pretty tedious reading.

You also risk conveying an impression of arrogance and egocentrism: 'I this . . .', 'I that . . .', 'I the other . . .', 'me, me, me!'

It might not be easy to cut down on your use of 'I', but you should definitely make an effort to do so. Look at each sentence that begins with 'I' and see whether you can rephrase it so that it starts with a different word.

If you can turn round a sentence so that it starts with 'You' or 'Your' then this is ideal, because it shows your focus is on the reader, not on yourself.

Further advice on writing style is included in Chapter 1, page 23: Content and style: what to say and how to say it.

11 Lack of coherent structure

make sure your letter is structured in a logical fashion

Like all the best stories, the best letters have a strong – and clearly defined – beginning, middle and end. It's important to make sure your letter is structured in a logical fashion. Capture their attention, make an impact, maintain their interest and finish with a strong closing paragraph.

You've only got a certain amount of space – and a certain number of words – to get your message across. If you don't structure your letter carefully then you'll end up rambling – and the impact of your letter will be severely diluted.

12 Too long

As a general rule, most cover letters don't – and shouldn't – exceed one A4 page in length. Never lose sight of the fact that your cover letter is not intended to take the place of your CV – it's meant to act as an introduction.

Unless there are clear instructions to the contrary, you should aim to keep your letters short and sweet. A handful of paragraphs are normally more than sufficient to whet the recruiter's appetite and entice them to read your CV.

If you find your letter is spilling over on to a second page then take a look at Chapter 1, page 34: Content and style: what to say and how to say it.

13 Failing to spot linguistic errors

 **brilliant** statistic

Our research has shown that 60 per cent of cover letters contain linguistic errors.

It might seem obvious. It might seem hard to believe that people actually do send out letters with errors in them. But, believe me, it happens all the time – so if you can make sure that your letters are totally error-free, you will immediately be at an advantage.

It is essential to check – and double-check – that there aren't any spelling or grammatical errors, as this is most likely the recruiter's first impression of you. Make sure it's a positive one.

brilliant blooper

In one unfortunate case, the individual in question got very confused about the difference between 'role' and 'roll'. He kept referring throughout both his cover letter and his CV to the various 'rolls' he had had – for example, 'an important roll in the finance department', 'sharing a roll with another colleague' and so on.

For the full story on spelling, grammar and typos, please refer back to Chapter 1, page 27: Content and style: what to say and how to say it.

14 Spamming everyone with the same letter

In just the same way that your CV should ideally be tailored for each application, so should your cover letter. In fact, it is even more important to tailor your letter. A carefully targeted letter can easily mean the difference between success and failure.

It is astonishing how many people use exactly the same cover letter and exactly the same CV for every single application.

It stands to reason that every job and every organisation is different and every cover letter should therefore also be subtly different. If you send the same letter to everyone, changing only a few minor details such as the recipient's name and address, then your chances of success will most definitely fall considerably.

I cover more about the importance of tailoring your applications in Chapter 1, page 35: Content and style: what to say and how to say it.

15 Not signing the letter

Whilst you won't be able to physically sign a letter sent by email, you should always sign letters sent by post or by fax.

It's a minor detail, but an important one.

By taking the time to sign the letter before sending it, you're giving out one further signal to the reader that you have taken the time to write to them personally – and haven't just sent out the same letter to dozens of people.

By adopting a personalised approach, you stand a much better chance that the recipient will take the time to listen to what you have to say for yourself.

16 Failing to send a cover letter at all

Yes, I know I said this chapter would cover the 15 most common CV writing mistakes, but everyone loves a bonus, don't they?

So, here's a sixteenth mistake for you: failing to include a cover letter at all.

You would be surprised how many people think they can just send their CV off on its own and don't need to bother with a cover letter. Whilst I'm not saying this will never work, I can say that it will rarely work, and I believe I have firmly demonstrated how much a cover letter can do to improve your chances of success.

If you're going to go to the trouble of sending off your CV then it's always worth taking a little bit more time to construct a brilliant cover letter to go with it.

Never send a CV without a cover letter unless you are specifically told to do so.

CHAPTER 7

Other job search letters

Application follow-up letters

It's astonishing how many people assiduously send off application after application but do precisely nothing to follow up on these when they do not receive a response. However, following up on the applications you send can considerably increase the number of interviews to which you are invited.

As you have no doubt realised, it can take a lot of time, work and effort to put together a compelling application. Having gone to all that trouble, why not go the extra mile and follow up on applications that haven't resulted in a response? Writing a follow-up letter is very quick and easy by comparison to writing your original letter and, given the effect it can have on a recruiter, is more than worth the little bit of extra effort. It can really underline your interest in working for them.

Following up on speculative applications

It should be noted that there is generally not much point in following up on speculative applications. A speculative application is, by its very nature, a hit and miss affair. You can expect that the majority of recipients won't bother replying – and you shouldn't be bothered about following up either. It's unlikely to get you any further forward and could even have a negative effect.

The exception would be if you are still keen to work for them several months after sending your original letter and actually have something to add to your original application – for example, a new qualification.

Following up on advert-response letters

Advert-response letters are different though. I would always recommend following up on each and every one of them, although it's probably safest to leave at least a couple of weeks from when you sent the original letter – or a week from the closing date quoted in the advert (if indeed one was quoted).

You can largely base your follow-up letter on your original letter to them. Take your original letter, save it under a new filename and just edit the core text.

---

brilliant case study

The first paragraph of Joe's letter might now read:

> I recently submitted my CV for the position of Senior Sales Manager. As I have not yet received a response to my application, I would like to confirm that you have indeed received it; I would emphasise that I remain very interested in the position.

You can follow this introduction with a key sales point, by simply trimming down the central paragraphs from your original letter. And you do of course want to conclude your letter with a suitable call to action.

---

brilliant case study

> I would be more than happy to resubmit my application if necessary. Please do not hesitate to call me on 07700 900 159 so as to arrange this.

You could simply enclose a further copy of your CV. However, concluding your letter with the above-mentioned call to action is more likely to prompt the reader to pick up the phone and speak to you – and that will work very much to your advantage.

After all, it's unlikely they didn't receive your original application. It's more likely they just haven't dealt with it yet. A quick rummage in their in-tray and they should be able to locate your CV.

An alternative approach is to pick up the phone and call the intended recipient yourself. Some experts (normally American) do recommend this as an 'aggressive sales tactic'. However, put yourself in the recruiter's shoes – it's likely to be rather annoying, isn't it? Would you want candidates calling you out of the blue to nag you for a decision? By sending a letter, you get your point across without causing too much disruption to the recruiter's day.

Keeping track of your job hunt

I've put together a spreadsheet for you, to help you keep track of the applications you send out – who you've sent them to, what date, how you sent them (post/email/fax) and so on.

This tracking tool will help you to know whether and when to follow up on an application and, quite simply, will prevent you from becoming very confused! It's likely that you will need to send out dozens of applications to secure the job you want and it's easy to get in a mess. Much better to keep yourself organised – and this Excel spreadsheet will enable you to do just that.

It's even got functionality to subsequently track your interviews.

To download your free copy, please visit the following link: **http://www.ineedacv.co.uk/tracker**.

↗ **brilliant** case study

And here's Joe's finished application follow-up letter:

JOE BLOGGS

1 Anyold Road, Guildford AN1 1CV
Telephone: 01632 960 314 (Home); 07700 900 159 (Mobile)
Email: joebloggs@example.com

Mr. John Hammond
Sales Director
Boozy Direct Limited
Davidson Way
GUILDFORD   AN7 7CV

24 June 2009

Dear Mr. Hammond,

SENIOR SALES MANAGER VACANCY – REF. ABC123

I recently submitted my CV for the position of Senior Sales Manager. As I have not yet received a response to my application, I would like to confirm that you have indeed received it; I would emphasise that I remain very interested in the position.

In my current role, the sales campaigns I have devised and implemented have been successful both in developing existing buyer relationships and in generating valuable new business. I have delivered a substantial increase in weekly sales levels – from £45,000 to £85,000 – and believe I could make a very significant contribution to your own sales operation.

I would be more than happy to resubmit my application if necessary. Please do not hesitate to call me on 07700 900 159 so as to arrange this.

Yours sincerely,

Joe Bloggs

Interview thank-you letters

The goal of your speculative and advert-response letters is obviously to get your foot in the door for an interview. Having achieved that, it's easy to think that the matter is now out of your hands and that it's just a question of sitting back and waiting to see whether the interviewer decides to give you the job or not.

Wrong.

But that is precisely what 90 per cent of people do!

The importance of being proactive

At no stage in your job hunt should you be sitting back and waiting for anything – not until you've achieved the ultimate goal of receiving a job offer. In a tight job market you need to be proactive and constantly keep up your efforts to land a new job. You need to have a follow-up strategy in place.

> in a tight job market you need to be proactive

In exactly the same way that following up on your original application can boost your odds of success, so can following up immediately after an interview. You are writing, ostensibly, to thank the interviewer for their time, but actually you're aiming to seize one last opportunity to make an impact on them – to reiterate how your skills and experience meet their requirements.

Once you've got to the interview stage, the odds are already narrowing down very much in your favour. There could easily have been as many as 100 initial applicants. However, less than 10 are likely to have been invited for interview. Success is within your grasp, and one final effort at this stage can really swing things in your favour.

brilliant tip

You probably devoted a good few hours of your time to putting together your application and attending the interview – and yet it doesn't take more than 10 minutes to knock out a well-crafted thank-you letter.

Avoiding procrastination

Follow up as soon as you can after the interview, either the same day if possible or, at the latest, the next day. By the time a recruiter has reached the interview stage, decisions can be made very quickly. You need to get your final shot in there before it's too late.

All you need to produce is a brief letter thanking the interviewer for their time and re-confirming your interest in the post. You should subtly remind them at the same time as to how your skills and experience meet their requirements.

So few people take the time to do this that you will stand out in the interviewer's mind – at the very moment when they will be making a crucial decision concerning your future.

It won't guarantee you the job, but it can only help.

It will save time if you take your original letter to them as a base, although you may of course need to change certain details as the individual you originally contacted might not have been the person who actually interviewed you. And if you were interviewed by more than one person then send it to whichever one of them arranged the interview with you (or with the recruitment agency representing you).

brilliant case study

The start of Joe's letter looks like this:

> I am writing to thank you for taking the time to interview me on June 30th and to confirm my strong interest in the Senior Sales Manager vacancy. I would also like to reiterate the qualities which I believe make me ideally suited to the role:

You can follow this introduction with your key sales points extracted from the central paragraphs of your original letter. It is perfectly acceptable in this instance to use bullet points to put these points across in list form.

You can conclude your letter along the lines of:

brilliant case study

> I look forward to hearing from you once a decision has been reached. In the meantime, please do not hesitate to call me on 07700 900 159 should you require any further information.

This is a fairly straightforward example and you can, of course, expand on it if appropriate. You may have thought of an important point since the interview that might further support your case. You may be able to refer to something that the interviewer mentioned that was of particular interest. There are numerous possibilities, but don't go over the top; at the end of the day it's only really a thank-you letter.

Sometimes you just have to pick up the phone

If a week passes after sending this letter and you still haven't heard anything then don't be shy to telephone the organisation and enquire politely whether a decision has been reached. This isn't harassment; having gone to all the trouble of attending an interview, the least the organisation can do is let you know the outcome.

Unfortunately, not all organisations will bother to notify candidates of a negative decision. It's very bad etiquette – but disappointingly common.

brilliant case study

Here's an example of an interview thank-you letter that Joe sends:

JOE BLOGGS

1 Anyold Road, Guildford AN1 1CV
Telephone: 01632 960 314 (Home); 07700 900 159 (Mobile)
Email: joebloggs@example.com

Mr. John Hammond
Sales Director
Boozy Direct Limited
Davidson Way
GUILDFORD   AN7 7CV

30 June 2009

Dear Mr. Hammond,

SENIOR SALES MANAGER VACANCY – REF. ABC123

I am writing to thank you for taking the time to interview me on June 30th and to confirm my strong interest in the Senior Sales Manager vacancy. I would also like to reiterate the qualities which I believe make me ideally suited to the role:

- Highly experienced with a successful track record in sales management
- Proven capacity to deliver substantial increases in sales levels
- Able to develop existing buyer relationships and generate valuable new business
- Extremely commercially astute and adept at negotiating profitable contracts
- Outstanding communication and organisation skills, with a natural talent for PR
- High standard of both written and spoken French, having worked in France

I look forward to hearing from you once a decision has been reached. In the meantime, please do not hesitate to call me on 07700 900 159 should you require any further information.

Yours sincerely,

Joe Bloggs

Negotiating an offer

Congratulations! You've got a job offer on the table.

Whilst, in many cases, an employer might make a straightforward offer and you will be inclined to accept it without question, there will be occasions when you may wish to negotiate the precise details of their offer. If you're unprepared, this can be a difficult stage to handle. However, as always, if you've done your research and thought the matter through, your end goal is now very much in sight.

The package

There's a reason this section is called 'Negotiating an offer' and not 'Negotiating your salary'. It's because, depending on your circumstances, there could be a whole hoard of other factors you need to take into account besides just your salary.

- Cash: bonuses; profit-share; commission; overtime; staff discounts.
- Time: holiday allowance; time off in lieu.
- Sickness: sick pay.
- Car: company car; car allowance; car insurance.
- Training: training opportunities; training allowance.
- Medical benefits: private health insurance; dental plan; health club membership.
- Pension: pension plans; pension contributions.
- Childcare.
- Share options.
- Termination: notice period; 'gardening leave'; non-compete clauses.

In most cases, salary will be the most important item on your list – and is the main focus of this section – but you mustn't lose sight of other factors that constitute the total package. Depending on the nature of these 'extras', they could make a relatively low basic salary seem much more attractive.

You should also take into account the effect this job is going to have on your CV. If it's going to help you develop in ways that will be of significant value to you in your next job (and will consequently boost your next salary package), you may be prepared to accept a lower offer in order to secure the job – maybe even lower than you are currently earning.

Market research

The very first step you should take (and should have taken long before a formal offer comes your way) is to research the kind of package usually offered for the type of position for which you are applying. To put it another way, you need to establish your market value. It is vital for you to have a realistic idea of what you should be worth to the employer – and it's vital for you to have this before you even start looking for jobs.

you need to establish your market value

brilliant tip

If you're working with a recruitment consultant, they can normally help you with this. However, there is plenty of information to be gleaned through looking at other job adverts and by checking online.

Once you've established a range for your market value, you need to decide the following.

● What is the minimum that you would be prepared to accept, assuming the job is suitably attractive?

● What is the maximum you can reasonably expect to achieve without breaking the deal?

Only you can decide what the minimum is that you would be prepared to accept, but your research should make it clear what the maximum is that you are likely to achieve.

The salary question

We established in Chapter 3 that many job adverts will ask for details of your current – or expected – salary. Whilst your current salary is a matter of fact, my advice for handling a question about your expected salary was to dodge it slightly and quote a range of possibilities rather than give a precise answer. It's always best to wait until a firm job offer is being made before going into detail on this issue.

That time has now come.

Whilst you will now need to be specific as to your requirements, it remains important (with a few exceptions, e.g. money-driven and largely commission-based roles) to convey the impression that money is not the only deciding factor in your choice of a new job and a new employer. Instead, your emphasis should be on politely, but firmly, conveying that you are aware of your value and that you feel it is only appropriate that you should be remunerated accordingly.

If your prospective employer makes the first move
In most cases your prospective employer will make the first move and tell you what they are prepared to offer. This has both advantages and disadvantages. The main advantage is that they have shown their hand and you now know how close to (or far from) your own expectations their expectations are. The main disadvantage is that if their offer isn't sufficient then the onus is on you to make the next move.

If you are expected to make the first move
If an employer makes no specific offer but asks you to name your price then they're certainly putting you on the spot.

Your approach should be to try to identify whether or not they at least have a salary range in mind. An employer will normally have established such a range. However, if challenged to reveal it, they will probably err on the side of caution – so don't be immediately disappointed if your salary requirements exceed the range quoted.

The next move
Regardless of how the negotiations kick off, you should be aiming to pitch for a salary at the top end of the range – and consequently be prepared to negotiate and reduce that figure as necessary in order to reach a compromise. This is a standard haggling technique. Start high and be prepared to come down.

Bargaining strategies
The most important bargaining strategy at your disposal is to play this employer off against others. Politely point out that you have applications

in progress for other roles where the packages offered are more in line with your requirements – and that you would naturally expect this employer to be able at least to match these offers, if not improve upon them. Whether or not you have firm offers from anyone else is, to a degree, beside the point; the point is to reiterate your market value to the employer – and that you, entirely reasonably, expect to receive what you're worth.

If you're unable to adopt this strategy then your next best strategy is to come clean and state the market research you have undertaken, give the employer the salary range you have identified and then make your case as to why you feel the high end of that scale best reflects your worth. If you've reached this stage then you've clearly already made a strong case at interview – and the employer now wants you. This is to your advantage. However, you may still need to make a final pitch to secure the level of salary you desire.

Reaching agreement

Once you've both got your cards on the table, a discussion may follow. It may take compromises on both your parts in order finally to reach agreement.

There are so many different ways in which this conversation may unfold that it's impossible for me to provide you with a precise winning formula. For a start, you may be negotiating in person, via a recruitment consultant, by telephone or even in writing.

brilliant tip

Whatever happens, keep your cool and maintain a professional detachment. Don't let the discussions become at all heated, and demonstrate to the employer that you are willing to work with them to reach a mutually beneficial agreement. The confident manner in which you handle the negotiations may be sufficient grounds alone for the employer to feel you warrant more than their original offer.

The worst-case scenario

There's normally nothing to be lost in attempting to negotiate a higher salary than the employer originally offers. Provided you handle proceedings in a diplomatic fashion, the worst possible outcome is likely to be that the employer sticks to their guns and refuses to contemplate a higher offer. However, having come this far (recruiting is an expensive process) most employers will usually display at least a little flexibility. If they do refuse to budge then it's up to you to decide whether or not their offer is sufficient or whether you will have to reject it. Be warned that, if you do flat-out reject their offer, the chances of their increasing it at this stage will not be high.

Another possible downside to negotiating is that, feeling they have initially paid 'over the odds' for you, an employer might be rather ungenerous when it comes to reviewing your salary in the future. However, a bird in the hand is definitely worth two in the bush and, if an employer fails to give you the pay rises you deserve then you can always look elsewhere.

Considering the offer

Once the employer has made their final offer, you are under no obligation to accept it on the spot. It's entirely acceptable – and definitely recommended – to at least sleep on it. Such a major decision requires careful consideration and most employers will respect you for taking a little time to think it over.

Multiple and counter-offers

Another reason for taking at least 24 hours to consider an offer is that it will give you a chance to use this offer to influence others you may have received. If you've worked hard on your job hunt then it's not unusual to get to a position where you are confronted with multiple offers. Whilst there are obvious risks involved, you can attempt to play them off against each other so as to achieve an even stronger offer.

brilliant tip

Bear in mind that it's not just prospective employers who might make you a counter-offer. Your own current employer might well do so.

Get it in writing

Once you have reached final agreement, it is absolutely essential to get the offer in writing. This should confirm the precise details of the package being offered. It is vital to have this in hand before you contemplate resigning from your current position. I can't stress enough how important this is. A verbal offer can be withdrawn at any time and you could find yourself in a very difficult position.

> it is absolutely essential to get the offer in writing

It is worth noting that, in the UK, there is no legal requirement for a written contract of employment. A contract is deemed to exist the moment you accept a job offer. However, an employer is still required to give you (normally within two months of your start date) what is known as a 'written statement of employment particulars' detailing certain key terms of your employment.

Whilst a written offer on the employer's part is normally legally binding, it is common practice for it to be subject to suitable references. And that is the subject of the next section.

 **case study**

Joe isn't entirely happy with the initial salary he's been offered and decides to write to attempt to increase their initial offer:

JOE BLOGGS

1 Anyold Road, Guildford AN1 1CV
Telephone: 01632 960 314 (Home); 07700 900 159 (Mobile)
Email: joebloggs@example.com

Mr. John Hammond
Sales Director
Boozy Direct Limited
Davidson Way
GUILDFORD   AN7 7CV

7 July 2009

Dear Mr. Hammond,

SENIOR SALES MANAGER VACANCY – REF. ABC123

Thank you very much for your preliminary offer to join your team as Senior Sales Manager.

I enjoyed the discussions we had during my interviews and this position is definitely of particular interest to me.

However, the opportunities I'm currently pursuing generally involve salary packages between £35K and £40K – and your offer of £35,500 clearly falls at the low end of this spectrum.

Whilst the salary won't necessarily be the deciding factor in my choice, I would like to achieve a position which offers nearer the high end of this scale – a package which I feel best reflects my worth and my market value.

I would therefore respectfully request that you review your initial offer. Whilst I am happy with the other terms of your offer – company car, bonus scheme, etc. – I do consider the salary to be on the low side and would appreciate it if you could bring it more into line with other offers I am contemplating.

As you are aware, I am a highly motivated salesman and have, in my current role, delivered a substantial increase in weekly sales levels, from £45,000 to £85,000 – very nearly double. I believe I will be able to make a similar, significant contribution to your company which will more than warrant a slightly higher initial salary.

I am naturally keen that we should reach a mutually beneficial agreement on this. Please do not hesitate to call me on 07700 900 159 so that we might discuss the matter in greater depth.

Yours sincerely,

Joe Bloggs

Requesting a reference

Most offers of employment will be subject to your prospective employer being able to obtain satisfactory references. Indeed, some employers will withhold making an offer of employment until they have finished obtaining references.

Of course, not all employers will bother with this formality. With people being increasingly worried, for legal reasons, about giving anyone a bad reference, the whole references game can often seem a fairly pointless exercise. And it has been known for an individual's current employer to give them a glowing reference just because they are keen for them to leave!

Nevertheless, many employers will still pursue references, and in certain lines of work they can take the issue of references very seriously indeed.

Who to choose?

Traditionally, you are expected to be able to provide details of at least two referees – usually one 'professional' (your current or previous employer) and one 'personal' (often a former teacher or lecturer). However, it is not unheard of for a prospective employer to want to check not only with your current employer, but also with your previous employer and maybe even your employer before that. It all depends on how thorough they want to be – and how sensitive a role it is that you are being recruited for.

Whilst you could just dish out name and contact details on request, it is much better etiquette to contact your potential referees before releasing such details. Normally you won't have to worry about this until the interview – or even the offer – stage, but some employers will insist on having details of referees up front, as will some recruitment agencies. Generally, whilst the examples in this chapter assume Joe already has an offer on the table, it won't hurt for you to start getting in touch with potential referees early – before you've even reached the interview stage.

brilliant tip

Details of referees generally shouldn't be included on your CV. They're a waste of valuable space. They clutter it up and, more importantly, you will find that your referees get pestered unnecessarily by time wasters. By the time they have handled their umpteenth enquiry of the day, they are a lot less likely to say nice things about you! A simple statement at the bottom of your CV, saying 'References are available on request' is more than sufficient.

Very occasionally you may be expected to secure a formal written reference yourself, but in the vast majority of cases all you need to do is obtain permission to release your referees' contact details to any interested parties. Depending on your relationship with your referee, you may find it is quickest and easiest to just pick up the phone. However, in most cases a brief but courteous letter will be appreciated.

Requesting a reference from a previous employer

If you're looking to obtain a letter of recommendation from a previous employer then, provided you parted on good terms, it should be a relatively straightforward matter.

The tone you adopt in your letter will depend very much on your relationship with that employer. If your relationship with them was fairly formal then your letter should reflect that. Conversely, if you have perhaps remained friends with them outside of work then your tone could be a lot more relaxed.

Either way, you should ensure that you clearly state your phone number so that they can just pick up the phone to agree to your request. It'll normally be quicker and easier for them than their having to write back.

Requesting a reference from your current employer

Writing to request a reference from your current employer is somewhat more complicated than requesting a reference from a previous employer.

In most cases, if you're looking to leave your current employer then you're likely to remain fairly secretive about the fact. You're unlikely to want your current employer to know about it. It's a delicate matter.

You know the routine: having to invent excuses to skip off work for an interview, discreetly popping out of the office to take calls on your mobile from recruitment agencies and so on. Nobody likes to have to sneak around, but being furtive about your plans is frequently the best policy.

Ultimately, you will of course have to bite the bullet. And if your prospective new employer requires a reference from your current employer before they'll confirm their offer then it's definitely time to come clean and make your confession.

Letting your current employer know that you are looking for work elsewhere – and indeed asking them to help you achieve this – is obviously a little tricky. A lot will depend on what sort of individual your current employer is. If they're likely to react negatively then you'll want to make fairly sure that your prospective new employer is serious about wanting to hire you. It can be very uncomfortable staying on in a role once your employer knows that you would rather be working elsewhere. And a lot will also depend on how you phrase your request. A well-planned and carefully written letter can make all the difference.

After receiving such a letter, your current employer may very possibly try to negotiate to retain you – or at least want to discuss matters with you in detail to better ascertain precisely why it is that you wish to leave.

You might find they make an immediate offer of a pay rise and it can be tempting to accept such offers – but is money the only the reason you are looking for another job? Probably not. And how mercenary will you appear if you accept their offer? It could permanently damage your credibility in the eyes of your employer and sour your relationship in the long term. Clearly it is something you will need to think about very carefully. (I will also be discussing counter-offers in the next section.)

Requesting a 'personal' reference

The ways in which you might tackle a letter requesting a personal reference will vary widely according to the nature of your relationship with the individual concerned.

brilliant case study

Joe decides one of his former university lecturers would be a good choice for a personal reference. The following examples cover all three types of reference request letter.

Requesting a reference from a previous employer:

JOE BLOGGS

1 Anyold Road, Guildford AN1 1CV
Telephone: 01632 960 314 (Home); 07700 900 159 (Mobile)
Email: joebloggs@example.com

Mrs. Caroline Carey
Sales Director
Drinks Time Limited
Relativity Road
GUILDFORD   AN9 1CV

7 July 2009

Dear Caroline,

I do hope you are well and prospering.

I have recently applied for a job with Boozy Direct as a Senior Sales Manager, having been in my current position as Sales Manager for Stationary Stationers for the past couple of years since working with yourself.

My application has progressed well and they have now made me a provisional offer. However, before confirming their offer, Boozy Direct wish to take up references – both personal and professional.

I am therefore writing to ask if you would mind my providing them with your contact details as my previous employer. You are clearly well placed to provide a professional reference.

I look forward to hearing from you and thank you for your time. Please do not hesitate to call me on 07700 900 159 if you would like to discuss this further.

Kind regards,

Joe Bloggs

Requesting a reference from a current employer:

JOE BLOGGS

1 Anyold Road, Guildford AN1 1CV
Telephone: 01632 960 314 (Home); 07700 900 159 (Mobile)
Email: joebloggs@example.com

Mrs. Bryone Ingrid
Sales Director
Stationary Stationers Limited
Pencil Lane
GUILDFORD   AN4 6CV

7 July 2009

Dear Bryone,

After careful consideration, I have made the decision to explore other offers of employment and have consequently applied for a job with Boozy Direct as a Senior Sales Manager.

However, before confirming their offer, they would like to contact you for a reference. I am therefore writing to ask if you would mind my providing them with your contact details as my current employer.

I would like to state that I am very grateful for the opportunities with which you have presented me during the course of my employment with you and, should I be successful in my application with Boozy Direct, I will of course do my best to help ensure the seamless transfer of my duties and responsibilities before leaving.

I look forward to hearing from you and thank you for your time.

Kind regards,

Joe Bloggs

Requesting a 'personal' reference:

JOE BLOGGS

1 Anyold Road, Guildford AN1 1CV
Telephone: 01632 960 314 (Home); 07700 900 159 (Mobile)
Email: joebloggs@example.com

Dr. Hugh House
Senior Lecturer
The University of Somewhere
Academic Lane
SOMEWHERE   SO1 9ZZ

7 July 2009

Dear Dr. House,

I do hope you are well and prospering.

Following the completion of my BA (Hons.) in Marketing and Advertising, I have applied for a job with Boozy Direct as a Senior Sales Manager.

My application has progressed well and they have now made me a provisional offer. However, before confirming their offer, Boozy Direct wish to take up references – both personal and professional.

I am therefore writing to ask if you would mind my providing them with your contact details. You are clearly well placed to provide a personal reference.

I look forward to hearing from you and thank you for your time. Please do not hesitate to call me on 07700 900 159 if you would like to discuss this further.

Yours sincerely,

Joe Bloggs

Resignation letters

There are of course various different ways of approaching the resignation process, some right and some wrong. You might be leaving your current employer but it never hurts to leave them with a positive impression of you.

There are only two points you really have to get across when writing your letter of resignation – namely:

- the fact that you're resigning;
- your acceptance that you are (probably) bound by a notice period.

Anything else is just a nicety. But it's well worth being as nice as possible about the matter.

harsh words in a resignation letter could easily come back to haunt you

Harsh words in a resignation letter could easily come back to haunt you in the future – not least if you ever need a reference from this employer.

Why are you leaving?

They are of course going to be wondering why you're leaving. The important thing is to realise that you're under no obligation to go into any details. In fact, you're under no obligation to give any reason at all. You could simply tell them you've decided the time is right to 'move on to a new challenge'. Whilst they might be curious to know more, discretion will prevent many employers from prying any further.

 **brilliant** case study

> After careful consideration, I have made the decision to move on to a new challenge

Don't burn your bridges

Make the effort to thank your employer for the opportunities they have given you and wish them the best for the future. Keep it very simple and businesslike whilst at the same time avoiding being cold and distant. There is nothing to be gained by burning bridges. You certainly shouldn't make any derogatory or disparaging comments about the organisation – or any other employee of the organisation.

 **brilliant** case study

> I would like to thank you for your support over the past two years and take this opportunity to wish the company the very best for the future.

You may find it hard to resist voicing particular concerns. However, whether or not your comments are justified, using your letter of resignation to launch a personal attack or to attempt to score points is highly ill-advised. Your intention may simply be to make your employer aware of a particular problem, but such a letter can nonetheless end up sounding vindictive – and is unlikely ever to do you any good.

Notice periods

In most jobs you will be bound by a period of notice, stipulated in your contract of employment. You should study your contract carefully so as to be aware of precisely what this period of notice is.

You should also identify how many leave days you remain entitled to, as these could reduce your notice period.

Whilst you are not under any legal obligation to give more than this statutory period of notice, in certain circumstances you may wish to do so. If this is the case then this should be made clear in your letter – with a statement indicating precisely when it is you wish to leave.

Don't delay!

Resignation letters should generally be sent as soon as possible after you have reached a firm decision to leave. Your decision only becomes legally binding on delivery of your letter of resignation. It should be noted that you don't need to post your letter – email is also legally binding.

Exit interviews

Upon receipt of an employee's resignation, many employers will wish to conduct what is known as an 'exit interview'. During such an interview, they may try to probe your reasons for leaving in greater detail, ostensibly to identify improvements they might be able to make to the working environment or to specific practices and procedures.

 **tip**

As with your original letter, keep your comments at an exit interview professional, not personal. Remember that an employer can't force you to disclose your reasons. Don't let yourself be talked into a corner. Whilst you may have kept your cool in your letter, it can be harder to do so face to face.

Counter-offers

Your employer may try to encourage you to stay with them, so you need to be prepared to face the possibility that they might offer you an improvement to the salary package they currently offer.

You might well be very tempted to accept such an offer and so it is important to remember your specific reasons for wanting to resign in the first place. Was money really your main motivator?

They may even offer you a promotion or a move to a different branch or department. This sort of counter-offer will take more serious thought on your part. How does the new job they are offering compare to the one you are planning to go to?

Whilst I'm not saying you shouldn't give serious consideration to counter-offers – and in some cases accept them – I would say that you should proceed with caution.

Maintaining contacts

The contacts you have made in your current job – including your colleagues – could be very useful to you later in your career, maybe even in your very next job. Make sure you keep details of names, contact numbers and email addresses.

 **brilliant** case study

Joe's finished resignation letter looks like this:

JOE BLOGGS

1 Anyold Road, Guildford AN1 1CV
Telephone: 01632 960 314 (Home); 07700 900 159 (Mobile)
Email: joebloggs@example.com

Mr. Drummond Chiles
Managing Director
Stationary Stationers Limited
Pencil Lane
GUILDFORD   AN4 6CV

14 July 2009

Dear Drummond,

RESIGNATION

In accordance with the terms of my contract of employment, please accept this letter as formal written confirmation of my resignation as Sales Manager with Stationary Stationers.

After careful consideration, I have made the decision to move on to a new challenge, following of course completion of my period of notice.

I would like to state that I am very grateful for the opportunities with which you have presented me during the course of my employment with you and I will of course do my utmost to help ensure the seamless transfer of my duties and responsibilities before leaving.

I would like to thank you for your support over the past two years and take this opportunity to wish the company the very best for the future.

Kind regards,

Joe Bloggs

Offer acceptance letters

It's clearly excellent news to receive a formal written offer for the job you want – and I'm delighted for you.

You do of course now need to write back to officially accept the offer – normally as soon as you possibly can. Whilst this will be one of the simpler letters you have to prepare, it is still worth taking the time to get it right and to continue to build a positive and professional image.

Like all letters, we can break down an offer acceptance letter into a series of modules and deal with them one by one.

But, first of all, you need to know who exactly you are writing to.

Who are you writing to?

By the time you receive a formal written offer, you could very possibly have dealt with quite a number of different people at the organisation.

Your offer may have been sent by someone you already know, or it may be sent by someone you've never heard of – for example, an HR assistant.

When accepting the offer you should always write back to the precise individual who sent you the offer, whether you know them or not. However, if there is somebody else you have dealt with who you feel should be kept informed – for example, your future boss – then you are certainly entitled to send them a copy letter.

Please refer back to Chapter 1, page 12: Structure: building your skeleton letter, for specific advice on handling copies.

'Thank you'

Whilst the main purpose of your letter is to confirm your acceptance of their offer, the very first line should deal with something almost as important – to thank the employer for their offer.

This is very simple, but it will be very much appreciated.

You should also make it clear what offer you are referring to. You should definitely quote the specific job title and, if appropriate, you can also quote any reference number(s) you know the employer to use (for example, from the original job advert).

 **case study**

> Thank you very much for your offer to join your team as Senior Sales Manager.

'I accept'

Your official acceptance of their offer is easy enough to convey and can be achieved in one short sentence.

 **case study**

> I am delighted to formally confirm my acceptance.

That's all you need to say for your acceptance to be legally binding.

Your start date

The precise date on which you are expected to start your new job should normally have been established by this stage. You will have identified what notice period (if any) you are currently bound by and, with the security of a firm written offer in your hand, you may well have already tendered your resignation from your current role.

Your start date will possibly have been mentioned by the employer in their offer letter and should certainly have been specified in any contract they enclosed.

All you need to do in your letter is confirm this date so that everyone knows where they stand.

> I can further confirm a start date of 1ˢᵗ September 2009 as previously agreed.

It's generally sufficient just to confirm the date; there's normally no need to state a precise time that you will arrive.

The personal touch

The case studies here are examples of all you really need to say to confirm your acceptance of a job offer. However, whilst it wouldn't necessarily be rude, it would certainly make for a fairly dry letter if this was all you had to say for yourself!

it never hurts to continue to demonstrate your enthusiasm for the role

Even though the job is in the bag it never hurts to continue to demonstrate your enthusiasm for the role – and to express how much you are looking forward to getting stuck in.

> I enjoyed the discussions we had during my interviews. As I stated, this position is of particular interest to me and I believe I will be able to make a significant contribution to your company. I very much look forward to commencing my new role in due course and thank you again for this opportunity.

Contracts

If your prospective employer has enclosed contracts for you to sign (normally two copies of the same contract – one for you and one for them), you should read through these carefully to make sure you are entirely in agreement. Errors do occur. In particular, if you've re-negotiated their original offer then you need to make sure this is fully reflected in the contracts they've sent.

If there is any aspect of your contract that you are unsure of then a quick phone call should be able to resolve it. If a mistake has been made then they can get replacement copies out to you without further delay.

Assuming you are fully in agreement, you normally only need to sign and date the contracts before enclosing one or both copies (depending on the instructions you've been given) with your acceptance letter. However, some employers may also require you to initial each individual page.

Don't forget to list any enclosures at the bottom of your letter using either 'enc.' or 'encs.', as discussed in Chapter 1, page 12: Structure: building your skeleton letter.

As noted earlier, in the UK, there is no legal requirement for a written contract of employment. A contract is deemed to exist the moment you accept a job offer. However, an employer is still required to give you (normally within two months of your start date) what is known as a 'written statement of employment particulars' detailing certain key terms of your employment.

Any other business

You may still have questions you need answered, such as precisely which individual or department you are expected to report to on your first day. However, I'd recommend you avoid getting into such matters in your acceptance letter. It's probably much easier just to pick up the phone. Even if you do raise such issues in your acceptance letter, the chances are that the employer will just call you to give you the answers – so why not pre-empt this and call them?

Conversely, your employer might themselves have raised further questions in their offer letter. It is, for example, not uncommon for an employer to ask whether you have (or will have) claimed any state benefits within the 57-day period prior to the start of your employment. If they do pose any such questions then you should of course answer them to the best of your ability.

 case study

Putting it all together, here is Joe's finished letter:

JOE BLOGGS

1 Anyold Road, Guildford AN1 1CV
Telephone: 01632 960 314 (Home); 07700 900 159 (Mobile)
Email: joebloggs@example.com

Mr. John Hammond
Sales Director
Boozy Direct Limited
Davidson Way
GUILDFORD   AN7 7CV

14 July 2009

Dear Mr. Hammond,

SENIOR SALES MANAGER VACANCY – REF. ABC123

Thank you very much for your offer to join your team as Senior Sales Manager.

I am delighted to formally confirm my acceptance.

I can further confirm a start date of 1st September 2009 as previously agreed. Please find enclosed my signed contracts of employment.

I enjoyed the discussions we had during my interviews. As I stated, this position is of particular interest to me and I believe I will be able to make a significant contribution to your company. I very much look forward to commencing my new role in due course and thank you again for this opportunity.

Yours sincerely,

Joe Bloggs

encs.: Contracts of employment

Rejecting an offer

What?! After all this effort, why on Earth would you want to reject an offer?

Whilst you might have experienced a sudden change in your personal circumstances, the most common reason for wanting to reject an offer is – because you've been fortunate enough to get an even better offer!

Maybe you've received two (or more) job offers simultaneously and one of them appeals to you more. Or possibly your current employer has promoted you or come in with a surprise pay rise.

Alternatively, you might have thought things through carefully and decided that, whilst the vacancy had initially seemed ideal, it isn't on reflection what you are really looking for – or doesn't provide the salary package you require. Perhaps you got a bad feeling about your prospective future line manager when you met at interview. There are many possibilities.

Why bother writing?

Whatever the precise reason, it is very important to write an appropriate letter immediately to decline any offers you won't be pursuing any further. This is more than a common courtesy; it is yet another step in building a strong reputation for yourself as a serious and professional individual. You could easily find yourself dealing with this organisation again, later in your career. Ensure you leave them with the best possible impression of you.

Clearly they've invested a lot of time and effort into dealing with you. They're consequently going to expect some sort of reason for you rejecting their offer – and you're going to have to give them one.

Why are you rejecting their offer?

You might have felt your prospective future line manager was cold and distant when you met at interview. You might have felt the salary offer was a joke. You might feel that your future career prospects would be limited within this particular organisation. But is it really going to be to your advantage to tell them any of that? It might make you feel better, but it isn't going to do anything to increase your standing in their eyes. You should always be very careful of projecting any negative emotion into a letter.

The best solution is often simply to tell them you've decided to 'pursue an alternative opportunity'. This might not fully satisfy their curiosity but at least it shouldn't overly offend them.

 **brilliant** example

I regret that, after very careful reflection, I have decided to pursue an alternative opportunity.

You should always bear in mind that you might end up dealing with this same organisation again at some stage. If they've made you an offer then they obviously have a positive impression of you – and you want them to maintain that.

How will they react to your letter?

It is always possible that, after receiving such a letter, they might try to negotiate the matter with you. They might, for example, immediately increase the salary package they are offering.

Only you can be the judge of whether or not to accept any revised offer they might make. I would, however, warn you that, if an employer ends up being forced to pay more for a new employee than they would initially have liked to, it can mean you could be waiting a long time for your first pay rise . . .

⟶ **brilliant** case study

Here's an example of a letter Joe sends to turn down a job he's no longer interested in:

JOE BLOGGS

1 Anyold Road, Guildford AN1 1CV
Telephone: 01632 960 314 (Home); 07700 900 159 (Mobile)
Email: joebloggs@example.com

Mr. Clarence Kavanagh
Sales Director
Foody Foody Limited
Catsin Road
GUILDFORD   AN3 5CV

14 July 2009

Dear Mr. Kavanagh,

SALES MANAGER VACANCY – REF. XYZ789

Thank you for your letter of July 12th.

I appreciate your having taken the time to interview me. However, I regret that, after very careful reflection, I have decided to pursue an alternative opportunity and will regrettably be forced to decline your offer.

Please do feel free to keep my details on file for future reference. I would be delighted to be informed should any similar vacancies arise in the future.

I enjoyed our discussion at my interview and I wish you and your organisation all the best.

Yours sincerely,

Joe Bloggs

Accepting rejection

It is a sad fact of life that, no matter how capable, qualified and experienced you are, most of the applications you make will result in rejection at one stage or another and for one reason or another. So you had better get used to it! Nearly everybody suffers a few such setbacks when they are hunting for a new job; many job hunters are regularly shot down in flames. Remember: it just wasn't your destiny.

Naturally, it can be very demoralising if you had your heart set on a particular opportunity. You have been through the highs and lows of being invited to a first interview and then to a second – or maybe even to an assessment centre – only to find out that at the end of the day the job went to someone else and all your efforts were for nothing.

Or were they?

Never say never

Your initial reaction to receiving a rejection from a prospective employer might be, if you're a philosophical sort of person, to conclude that it's the end of this particular road and that you need to turn your attentions to other possibilities you've got on the go.

However, call me stubborn, but I – and many other recruitment professionals – still recommend following up on such a rejection with, you've guessed it, yet another letter.

Allow me to explain why.

- You have quite probably worked pretty hard to get to this stage.
- They don't want to hire you now but they may well be interested in the future.
- It should only take you five minutes to fire off this one final letter.

Building bridges

Having taken the time to build bridges with this organisation, you'd be as well to maintain those bridges as best you can. You never know when your contacts might come in handy later in your career.

- You might end up getting a job where you deal on a regular basis with this organisation.

- You may have missed out on the current vacancy but they could have another one in just a few weeks' time.

- What if the person who won the job subsequently turns it down?

brilliant tip

Having invested this much in your relationship, it makes sense to seize the opportunity to spend a few more minutes developing that relationship even further.

Maintaining a positive attitude

The way you approach writing this letter is very important. You might feel a degree of resentment for having been made to jump through lots of hoops only for them ultimately to disappoint you – but you certainly don't want that kind of negative emotion to come through in your letter.

There isn't (or at least there shouldn't be) anything personal about their decision. 'It's just business.' They are not rejecting you as an individual – they are rejecting your candidature for this particular vacancy. In many cases theirs could be an extremely arbitrary decision; if you're faced with a number of high quality candidates then it can be very hard to choose between them. Indeed, sometimes there is so little to choose between candidates that, more than anything, success or failure is down to luck.

It is of course fine to express your disappointment, but you should definitely avoid sounding bitter! A negative attitude is unlikely to make a good impression.

> a negative attitude is unlikely to make a good impression

You should instead attempt to extract some constructive feedback from them so as to help you with future applications you make. Most recruiters won't volunteer this information – you'll have to ask them for it. You might just get back the usual canned response that 'it was an extremely difficult decision' and so on. You might get no reply whatsoever. But you might just get some really useful advice that could enable you to address any weaknesses or rectify any mistakes, so that you have a greater chance of success the next time round.

Down but not out

You're also demonstrating that you're somebody who doesn't like to lose and who will do their utmost to make sure they're less likely to lose out again in the future.

Above all else, remember that there is a job out there with your name on it. If no one has yet recognised your star quality then it's up to you to dazzle them!

 **brilliant** case study

This is how Joe handles rejection:

JOE BLOGGS

1 Anyold Road, Guildford AN1 1CV
Telephone: 01632 960 314 (Home); 07700 900 159 (Mobile)
Email: joebloggs@example.com

Mr. William Campbell
Managing Director
Drink Up Fast Limited
Longwinding Road
GUILDFORD   AN4 8CV

17 June 2009

Dear Mr. Campbell,

SALES DIRECTOR VACANCY – REF. LMN456

Thank you for your letter of June 15th.

I am naturally disappointed not to have been offered the post of Sales Director, although I do of course understand that the calibre of applicants was very high and reaching a final decision was not easy for you.

I appreciate your having taken the time to consider my application and I would of course be extremely grateful if you were able to give me any feedback on my application and on my performance at interview. I am keen to identify and resolve any weak points which may be impeding my progress. Any advice would be very welcome.

Finally, please do feel free to keep my details on file for future reference. I would be delighted to be informed should any similar vacancies arise in the future.

I enjoyed our discussion at my interview and I wish you and your organisation all the best.

Yours sincerely,

Joe Bloggs

Summary

- Following up immediately after an interview can significantly boost your odds of success.

- So few people take the time to do this that you will stand out in the interviewer's mind – at the very moment when they will be making their crucial decision.

- When resigning, it never hurts to leave your employer with a positive impression of you. It's well worth being as nice as possible about the matter.

- Aim to follow up on all rejections with a brief letter asking for constructive feedback.

- Remember that there is a job out there with your name on it. If no one has yet recognised your star quality then it's up to you to dazzle them!

CHAPTER 8

Career development letters

Whilst the majority of cover letters you write will be related to your hunt for a new job, there will be times when you need to write to try to improve upon the conditions of your current employment.

The two principal scenarios are:

- you want to request a pay rise;
- you want to request a promotion.

First, we're going to deal with how to successfully handle a request for a pay rise. We'll come to handling a request for a promotion later in the chapter.

Pay rise request letters

Requesting a pay rise

If you're happy in your current role and the only reason you would want to change jobs is that you feel you should be paid more, your first step should always be to address this issue with your current employer. There is every chance that a mutually agreeable solution can be reached.

There is no shame in asking for a pay rise. Whilst your employer might not be delighted by the prospect, they should respect that you are entirely within your rights to make such a request. If you feel you're no longer being paid what you're worth then you're perfectly entitled to speak up and say so. Ultimately, you could be doing your employer a favour. Rather than looking elsewhere for work and then just handing in your resignation, you are giving them a chance to review your remuneration and make an appropriate effort to retain your services.

there is no shame in asking for a pay rise

I won't claim that they'll greet your request with open arms though!

Timing

Before we talk about the content of your letter, let's discuss the timing of it. Timing can be a very important factor when asking for a pay rise. It can have a significant impact on your chances of success.

Clearly it would be a mistake to demand a pay rise too soon after starting a new job (or too soon after your last pay rise). You need to allow yourself time to make sufficient impact as would warrant a pay rise. Conversely, you shouldn't leave it too long either. You deserve to be paid what you're worth and not have your remuneration eroded by inflation.

Many organisations automatically review salaries on an annual basis. However, if 12 months pass and there's no sign that a pay rise is forthcoming then it's very possibly time for you to seize the initiative.

You still need to choose your moment carefully though. Try to pick a time when your contribution to the organisation is going to be seen in the best possible light. If you're halfway through a major project then wait until its successful completion. If you're working on a tender for a big contract then wait until you've won the contract. If you've recently taken on new duties or responsibilities then wait until you've demonstrated that you have risen to the challenge.

You also need to bear in mind other factors that could impact on the timing of your request. If your organisation is currently experiencing financial difficulties then your request may well be frowned upon. If your boss is under an unusual amount of stress – or is experiencing personal problems of some sort – then, again, you would be well advised to postpone your request until things have settled back down.

Tact and diplomacy

It's obvious enough that putting in a request for a pay rise can be a delicate matter.

Whilst receiving a letter of resignation is undoubtedly worse for an employer, receiving a request for a pay rise is not exactly good news either. A lot therefore depends on how precisely you write your letter and phrase your request.

I'm not just talking about your chances of successfully negotiating the pay rise; I'm also – and perhaps more importantly – talking about the relationship you have with your current employer.

If you get your letter right then it's not going to guarantee you a pay rise, but it will at least minimise the chances of your damaging your relationship with your employer in any way.

Whilst it's fine to have confidence in yourself – and in your right to make such a request – you should definitely avoid coming across as demanding. If you're asking for more money then the onus is clearly on you to make a persuasive case – but do act respectfully at all times.

Proving your value

Simply asking for more money for doing the same job is generally unlikely to go down well with an employer. Instead, you need to try to demonstrate to the employer the contribution you make to their organisation over and above their core expectations. You need to demonstrate what you've achieved. You need to demonstrate what you're really worth.

> you need to demonstrate what you're really worth

- What progress have you made since you started your current role (or during the course of the past year)?
- What value do you add to the organisation which warrants a higher level of remuneration?
- What examples can you cite to back up your claims?

The answers to these questions will be different for everyone. You need to think through your own answers – clearly and concisely – because they will be fundamental to the 'pitch' you make in your letter. Only by proving your value can you hope to prove your case for a rise.

You might think it should be blatantly obvious to your boss what you've achieved – but don't count on it! You still need to spell out your case in writing nonetheless.

What to ask for

What exactly do you want to ask for in your letter?

You could of course state the precise number of pound notes you're expecting. However, I wouldn't recommend this strategy.

The best approach is, having preliminarily made your case, to request a face-to-face meeting. This will give both you and your employer the opportunity to enter into a two-way dialogue, lay all your cards on the table and, with a bit of luck, reach a solution you are both happy with.

I would suggest you take a few minutes to read through Chapter 7, page 133: Negotiating an offer, so as to acquaint yourself with the basics of such negotiations. Whilst not all of the advice is relevant to this situation, a lot of the basic principles remain the same.

Avoiding threats

The thought of backing up your request with a threat might not even have crossed your mind. However, many employees – rather ill-advisedly – believe it to be a good negotiating tactic to threaten that they might be 'forced' to look for another job if their request isn't accepted. Such threats might be made very directly or they might just be subtly implied. But my advice is to make sure you don't make any threat of any sort.

Nobody likes to be threatened and an employer might well see this as blackmail – something they definitely won't respond to favourably. Yes, it's conceivable they may give in to this in the short term, but in the long term your relationship with them will be permanently scarred.

Your letter should focus very much on what you currently do for your employer, not what you will do if they fail to give you what you want.

Here's an example for you.

 example

Joseph Oladimeji

4 Anyold Road, London AN1 1CV ::: 07700 900 333 ::: joladi@example.com

Mr. Malcolm Smith
IT Director
The CV Centre Limited
Davidson Way
ROMFORD RM7 0AZ

17 June 2009

Dear Malcolm,

REMUNERATION REVIEW REQUEST

I am writing to request the opportunity for a review of my current remuneration.

It has now been just over a year since I took up my role as the company's Web Developer. In that time, I feel that I have made a very significant contribution to the company which warrants a reconsideration of the salary package I currently receive.

The systems I have put in place to collect potential sales leads online make a major contribution to the results of the sales team – these days more and more of our new business comes via the website. And, by identifying ways to attract potential new employees online, I have contributed to a reduction in the amount we spend on recruitment consultants – again resulting in a direct impact on the company's bottom line.

Most recently, I have completed an extensive site re-design which has seen our online sales conversion rate rise by approximately 17%. Since our marketing costs in this respect remain constant, the overall effect on profits is significant.

In view of the above, I would be grateful if we could timetable a meeting to discuss my role and my remuneration in greater detail.

I look forward to hearing from you and thank you for your time.

Kind regards,

Joseph Oladimeji

Promotion request letters

In many cases, the best way to progress to a more challenging role – a position with greater responsibility and autonomy – is to look for a new job. This is one of the top reasons why people want to change jobs.

However, this doesn't necessarily mean that your new job has to be with a different organisation. If you're happy working for your current employer but are simply no longer satisfied with the role you play in the organisation, the ideal situation could be to be awarded a promotion – rather than have to go through all the upheaval of moving to a different organisation.

Opportunities for promotion

You may already have identified a suitable vacancy in one of the following ways.

- Perhaps one has been advertised internally.
- Possibly someone in a more senior position has decided to leave or retire.
- Maybe a new branch, department or division is opening up.
- Your company could be tendering for a major new contract.

In such cases, your approach should not be too dissimilar to applying for any new job. Don't make the mistake of thinking that, just because you are already known to the organisation, you don't need to put together a comprehensive and compelling application.

The speculative approach

In many cases, however, you might not perceive a specific opportunity and may just be writing on a purely speculative basis. As such, there is of course no guarantee that a suitable position will be available with your current employer. A lot can depend on the size of the organisation, but it's definitely always worth a shot.

brilliant tip

Even if there isn't a position immediately available you will be demonstrating your desire to progress, and when a more senior position does become available your name could be first on the list. And in the meantime there's always the possibility that your employer might try to 'pacify' you with a pay rise!

One possibility is that your request will prompt your employer to seek ways in which they can change or add to your role so that you feel more fulfilled – with an accompanying pay rise, if appropriate.

From an employer's point of view, someone who wants a promotion is someone who is at risk of leaving unless you are able to find ways to accommodate their needs. One way or the other, if you're a valued employee, your employer is likely to make some effort to improve your situation.

Why do you deserve a promotion?

So, why exactly do you deserve a promotion? If it was just going to be handed to you on a plate then your employer would already have done so. No, you're going to need to justify your request – and you're going to have to do so persuasively. It's not too dissimilar to the kind of letter you would write to request a pay rise (see the previous section for pay rise request letters).

The main thrust of your letter should be to communicate to your employer how you have developed in ways that now warrant your promotion to a more senior position. The message you're sending is that you've mastered the requirements of your current role and, as a consequence, it is now no longer a sufficient challenge for you.

don't fall into the trap of underselling yourself

Don't fall into the trap of underselling yourself. Write your letter in the same style as you would if you were applying for a job with a different organisation. There's nothing wrong with blowing your own trumpet – because you can't rely on anyone else to do so!

Start with an overview of your time with the organisation and outline succinctly the progress you have made in that time. You should also make mention of any formal training you have undertaken since you were first appointed to the role.

Conclude by specifying the kind of role to which you would now hope to be appointed and politely invite the reader to discuss the matter with you in further detail.

Money, money, money

There is, initially, no need to bring up the subject of money when requesting a promotion. Your focus should be on your moving to a role that is more rewarding in and of itself, rather than just more rewarding in financial terms.

Most employers will be fully aware that, if they are to promote you, you will naturally be expecting an accompanying pay rise. However, this can be discussed later – possibly even after you have taken up your new role and have had a chance to prove yourself.

The following example should give you a good idea of what you should be aiming for when writing your own letter.

 example

Ashish Patel

5 Anyold Road
London AN1 1CV
Telephone: 01632 960 333
Mobile: 07700 900 666
Email: ashish@example.com

Mr. Paul Geary
Customer Services Director
The CV Centre Limited
Davidson Way
ROMFORD   RM7 0AZ

17 June 2009

Dear Mr. Geary,

PROMOTION REQUEST

I am writing to enquire whether there is any opportunity for my promotion to a more senior role.

Over the course of my past three years with the company, I believe I have developed my skills and experience in numerous different ways. I have matured as an individual and my experience of working with others – both colleagues and customers – has contributed a lot to my interpersonal skills. I am also better able to see the bigger picture and how the function of my department relates to the overall goals of the organisation.

Recently I have undertaken an evening course in business administration which has further helped to shape the way I work and has given a formal structure to many of the skills I have developed on a practical basis.

As a result of the above, I am now much more productive in my role – and much better equipped to help my colleagues to handle unusual or difficult situations. I therefore feel the time is right for me to step up to a management-level position and I would be pleased to discuss any opportunities which may be available.

I look forward to hearing from you and thank you for your time.

Yours sincerely,

Ashish Patel

Summary

- Whilst your employer might not be delighted by your asking for a pay rise, they should respect that you are entirely within your rights to make such a request.

- If you get your letter right then it's not going to guarantee you a pay rise, but it will at least minimise the chances of your damaging your relationship with your employer in any way.

- If you're no longer satisfied with the role you play in an organisation then the ideal situation could be to be awarded a promotion.

- You're going to need to justify your request by communicating to your employer how you have developed in ways that now warrant your promotion.

- Succinctly outline the progress you have made and be sure to make mention of any formal training you have undertaken since you were first appointed.

CHAPTER 9

From CVs to interviews . . .

CVs

'Curriculum vitae' is a Latin term and translates as 'the course of one's life'. The simplest dictionary definition says that a curriculum vitae is 'a summary of your academic and work history'. Well, that's basically true, but I see a curriculum vitae (commonly abbreviated, of course, to CV) as more of a personal sales brochure, one which should be very carefully written and presented to ensure you have the best possible chance of getting the job you want – to really showcase your talent.

It is not an autobiography. Simply writing down a list of everything you have done and everything you know will not guarantee you an interview. In fact, it will just bore the socks off the recruiter and undoubtedly count against you.

> the primary aim of your CV is purely and simply to win you an interview

You should never lose sight of the fact that the primary aim of your CV is purely and simply to win you an interview.

Laying the foundations: getting the basics right

It is vitally important to see matters from the recruiter's or prospective employer's perspective.

They're often faced with a pile of many hundreds of CVs to review – for just one vacancy. Almost a third of recruiters admit to only reading a CV for a minute before deciding whether to interview the candidate. In fact, many admit to spending even less time – 20 to 30 seconds is quite common.

They simply do not have the time to read them all in any depth. They're much more interested in getting out of the office and getting down the pub! In their initial sift, they will very likely be looking for reasons to discard your application, not for reasons to retain it. So how do you make your CV stand out? How do you maximise your chances of being amongst the 10 or so candidates they decide to invite for interview?

You need to determine exactly what to put in, exactly what to leave out and what kind of a 'spin' to put on your CV to ensure that yours will stand out from the competition. Getting it right is the difference between getting your foot in the door for an interview and ending up in the 'no thank you' pile – also known as the bin!

You need to help the recruiter as much as possible, as they see sifting through CVs as a chore and want it to be over as quickly as possible (remember, there's that pint waiting for them down the road!). They do not know you and they don't know what you're capable of – this is where you have to sell yourself.

The 15 most common CV writing mistakes – and how to avoid them

The CV Centre has conducted a comprehensive analysis of over 2,500 CVs to derive a 'top 15' of the common mistakes people make.

1 Inclusion of photographs

People often include photos of themselves on their CV. Don't! Unless you are applying to be a model or wish to work as an actor/actress then including a photo with/on your CV is definitely not recommended – at least not within the UK.

2 Inappropriate heading

Your CV should be headed with your name – and just your name – boldly and clearly, before any other details such as contact details and so on. It should not be headed 'Curriculum Vitae' or 'CV' or anything else. Just your name (and only your first name and your last name).

3 Missing or inappropriate email addresses

Whilst not having an email address at all on your CV is clearly a problem, it's not something I see very often. Far more common is the use of fun or jokey email addresses. Whilst these may be fine for corresponding with friends and family, employers will probably regard more 'serious' email addresses as simply more professional.

4 Superfluous personal details at the top of the CV

My clients often feel that it is compulsory to include details such as their marital status, nationality, number (and ages) of children/dependants and so on. Whilst, yes, it certainly used to be the norm to include this sort of information on a CV, it is now increasingly rare, given modern anti-discrimination legislation, to find these sorts of details on a CV. They simply aren't relevant.

5 Lack of clear section headings/separation of sections

It is vitally important for your CV to be easy for the reader to scan quickly. To this end, clear section headings and separation of sections is essential. I often recommend the use of lines or other graphic devices in this respect, although there are other ways of achieving a clearer separation.

6 Writing in the first person

The words 'I' and 'me' are often used repeatedly in homemade CVs. CVs should be written exclusively in the third person. Making a CV too personal by using 'I' and 'me' tends to look unprofessional. It can convey an impression of arrogance and egocentrism: 'I this ...', 'I that ...', 'I the other ...', 'me, me, me!' But most of all it's just too informal. It might seem unnatural to write a document about yourself and yet never use either 'I' or 'me', but recruitment experts conclusively agree that this is the best way to do it.

7 Lack of proper professional profile and/or objective

It is very important to include a sufficiently detailed and very carefully phrased professional profile and, if space permits, objective at the beginning of the CV. The reader needs to know instantly what you're about and what sort of position you are looking for. This is also a key area to consider tailoring for different applications. It's one of the first (and sometimes only) sections the reader will see and consequently gives you a vital opportunity to make a powerful first impression on them.

8 Inappropriate section order

It's extremely important to choose an appropriate order for the various sections of your CV. For example, the decision whether to put your education and qualifications before or after your career history is critical. It all depends on what is your greater selling point. You should make sure that all your most important information is conveyed on the first page – or, for a one-page CV, in the top half of the page.

9 No bullet pointing

In today's fast-paced world, recruiters no longer have the time to read large, solid blocks of prose. They need to extract the information they need – and they need to do it fast. Long paragraphs of prose are tiresome for a recruiter to read right through and, as a result, many simply won't bother. And this is where bullet pointing comes in, although, unfortunately, so many people fail to use it to their advantage within their CV.

10 Reverse chronological order not used

It is a standard convention on CVs to use reverse chronological order, i.e. to present your most recent information first, followed by older – and consequently less relevant – information. And I would strongly suggest you make sure your CV conforms to this.

11 Excessive details of interests

You should aim to keep your interests section brief. As with every other aspect of your CV, do include what you feel will count in your favour – but be selective about it. Many people write far too much in this section.

12 Date of birth included

I often get asked whether or not you should include your date of birth (or age) on a CV. The old answer to this used to be that you should include it, because recruiters expect to see it and so if you don't include it then it'll just draw attention to the fact. However, this advice has now changed – since the introduction of the Employment Equality (Age) Regulations 2006.

13 Referees included

Details of referees generally shouldn't be included on your CV. They're a waste of valuable space. They clutter it up and, more importantly, you will find that your referees get pestered unnecessarily by time wasters. By the time they have handled their umpteenth enquiry of the day, they are a lot less likely to say nice things about you!

14 Failing to spot linguistic errors

Our research has shown that 60 per cent of CVs contain linguistic errors. It is impossible to stress enough how important this issue is. Spelling and grammatical errors are amongst the most irritating errors a recruiter sees – and also amongst the most easily avoided. The answer is to check, check and check again.

15 Too long

This is one of the most common problems I see when people prepare their own CVs – they're quite simply too long. This is not an autobiography you're writing. It's a curriculum vitae. It's a lot shorter!

Five top tips to make your CV stand out

Make an effort to accommodate these five points when writing your CV and you'll immediately be well above average.

1 **Maximise readability.** It is essential for your CV to be easy for the reader to scan quickly and effectively. You need to separate different sections and insert clear section headings. Avoid long paragraphs; use bullet pointing to break up text into more manageable 'bite-size' chunks. It should be eye-catching and uncluttered. Check vigilantly for spelling and grammatical errors.

2 **Include professional profile and objective sections.** These sections should summarise and emphasise your key attributes and your intended future career path. Your words must flow seamlessly – avoiding cliché and superfluous hyperbole.

3 **Include achievements where possible.** If you can include an achievements section then it can make an instant and dramatic difference to the power of your CV, enabling you to distinguish yourself from other candidates.

4 **Keep your CV concise and to the point.** Your CV should be informative but also concise. In general, two A4 pages is a maximum. Too many CVs are quite simply too long. Only include information that will actually help to sell you. Recruiters don't want to waste time reading details irrelevant to your ability to fulfil the job role.

5 **Target/tailor your CV.** If possible, tailor your CV according to the specific vacancy for which you are applying. A carefully targeted CV can easily mean the difference between success and failure.

The CV Book

If you would like to learn more about CVs then please take a look at my comprehensive book on the subject, *The CV Book*. You can place an order for a copy via the following page on The CV Centre's website: **http://www.ineedacv.co.uk/thecvbook**.

Application forms

It's a fact of life that not every employer will accept a CV and cover letter. Many larger organisations – particularly those in the public sector – will have standardised recruitment systems whereby candidates are required to complete an application form.

One of the main reasons for an employer to use application forms rather than accept CVs is that it is considered to be easier – and fairer – when comparing one candidate to another. It levels the playing field. CVs and cover letters vary widely, from the brilliant right down to the outright absurd! However, by forcing every candidate to follow precisely the same format when presenting their details, the belief is that the quality of their CV and cover letter is no longer a deciding factor in the recruitment process.

Another reason employers give is that, because it is time consuming for a candidate to complete an application form, it reduces the number of applicants – in effect providing a form of pre-screening. The theory is that only those candidates who are really committed to the opportunity and who really think they have a chance will bother to take the time to apply.

Personally, I am not a fan of application forms; I am not convinced by the arguments employers put forward for using them. I believe that requesting a CV with an accompanying cover letter is the best way to initially screen candidates for almost any role.

However, since you will no doubt come up against application forms during your job hunt, this section is here to help you tackle them as successfully as possible.

Guidance notes

Your most useful tools when completing an application form will normally have been provided by the employer themselves.

Application forms are normally accompanied by some form of guidance notes, giving clear instructions as to what is expected of you. It is of the utmost importance that you follow any instructions to the letter.

> it is of the utmost importance that you follow any instructions to the letter

Application packs will also commonly include a job description and/or person specification. These will give you a very clear picture of exactly what it is the employer is looking for – enabling you to complete the form accordingly. This will also give you the opportunity to weigh up whether it is really worth your while applying for this job. Do you really meet their criteria? There really is very little point spending precious time completing an application form for a job you don't stand a good chance of getting.

You should also take careful note of the submission deadline or closing date. If you can't get your completed form to the employer before this deadline then don't bother taking this application any further.

The application form

Most application forms follow the same basic pattern and largely adhere to the same format as a traditional CV:

- Personal details
- Education and qualifications (including further training)
- Career history
- Interests and activities

In addition to these sections, most application forms have space for a 'personal statement' or ask a series of carefully designed 'competency questions'. This is normally the greatest challenge the form presents.

They may also ask for details of referees, as well as data required to ensure they adhere to their equal opportunities policy.

Below, we'll take a look at each of these sections, one by one.

Personal details

This is normally very simple. Answer each question clearly and accurately – making sure you don't accidentally miss a question. Depending on how well (or badly) designed the form is, it can be surprisingly easy to overlook a question.

Education and qualifications

Application forms normally require full details of all your qualifications including grades, and in the case of university degrees, often the specific modules you undertook. If your application progresses then you might find the employer asks for copies of your certificates, so it's obviously important to be as honest and accurate as possible when completing this section.

Whilst the format the employer has used may be geared towards UK qualifications, if your qualifications were gained abroad you should normally be able to make them fit. Many employers now use a qualification conversion table so, when assessing your application, they will be able to find the closest UK equivalents.

Career history

The level of detail required by the career history section varies widely from application form to application form.

Some forms will only request dates, job titles and organisation names. Others may want specific details of your duties, responsibilities and achievements – and maybe even your reasons for leaving.

If you're required to give a comprehensive description then do keep in mind the job description or person specification of the role for which you are applying. This is an important opportunity to demonstrate that you meet the criteria the employer has set out.

As with your CV, you will normally be expected to work in reverse chronological order.

Interests and activities

This should be very simple to complete and you can normally just copy details over from your CV. However, some forms might expect you to elaborate on your interests and activities more than you would normally do so when writing a CV.

Personal statement

This is undoubtedly the most important part of an application form – and the only part that is likely to cause you any real difficulty.

The first step – before you start writing – is to take a long, hard look at the job description and/or person specification. The onus is on you to demonstrate in your statement exactly how you meet the employer's criteria, so you need to make sure you understand very precisely what those criteria are.

It will help you to draw up a list of specific examples that you can use to illustrate the points you wish to make. Wherever possible you should try to integrate these real-world examples into your statement rather than just speaking hypothetically. Flagging up specific, relevant examples from your own experience is an ideal way of reinforcing your points in the reader's mind. You should be able to use your CV to help generate ideas, but don't be tempted simply to copy and paste.

When you come to putting pen to paper, either you can write using a paragraph structure as if you were writing a letter or you could try breaking up your statement using subheadings. Unless you are given instructions to the contrary, the choice is yours. However, whichever approach you use, ensure that your statement progresses in a logical, methodical and ordered fashion, tackling each of the key issues one by one.

brilliant tip

Try to remember that the personal statement is not your enemy; it is your big opportunity to sell yourself and really make an impact. Use positive, engaging language and try to inject some life into what can otherwise be a rather dry block of prose. Approach your application form in an enthusiastic frame of mind and it is sure to reflect in your style of writing.

You will often be limited as to the number of words you are allowed to use. However, by practising on a separate sheet (or word-processing document) first, you can make sure you adhere to this requirement.

Competency questions

As an alternative to the personal statement (and sometimes in addition), application forms may contain a series of carefully worded questions designed to assess and analyse certain key competencies – and to ascertain precisely why you are applying for the role.

In many ways, this is easier than completing a personal statement because the questions will steer you more precisely in the right direction. However, you should of course note that all applicants will have this same advantage.

In order to effectively handle such questions:

● read through the question carefully to make sure you have fully understood its meaning;

● think about your answer in detail before you start trying to write it down;

● ensure you cover all aspects of the question and don't miss anything;

● endeavour to back up your answers with appropriate examples from your own experience.

Referees

If an application form specifically asks for details of your referees then you will need to comply with this demand. Generally, you will be expected to provide details of at least two referees – usually one 'personal' and one 'professional'.

I would always recommend that you actually contact your potential referees before releasing their details. Not only do they need to be warned that they might be contacted, but it's also polite to ask for their permission to release their details.

It may be quickest and easiest just to pick up the phone, but in most cases a brief but courteous letter will be appreciated. I cover this in Chapter 7, page 140: Requesting a reference.

Miscellaneous formalities

Many employers now operate formal equal opportunities policies and, as part of this, you may be required to provide certain personal data regarding your ethnicity and so on. Make sure you complete such details in full. Rest assured that it is illegal for an employer to use such data when making their selection.

You may also be required to consent to the use of your data in accordance with the Data Protection Act.

On paper or online?

Some employers will issue their application forms on paper, others online – and some will give you the choice.

When completing an application form on paper:

- practise first using a photocopy so as to ensure your answers fit the space available;
- use a pen with black ink so that the employer can easily photocopy the form;
- write as neatly as possible – it's vital that your writing is easy to read;
- follow the instructions given and use block capitals where requested;
- don't forget to sign and date the form if you're asked to do so;
- take a photocopy of the completed form for use at interview.

When completing an application form online:

- keep a careful note of your log-in details if you're required to register first;
- type carefully – typing errors are not going to impress the reader;
- make sure you adhere to any word count restrictions that might be imposed;
- print a copy of the completed form for your records, if possible;
- keep a careful note of any reference number you are given on submission of your form.

Check and double-check

In just the same way that you should always very thoroughly check any CVs or letters you send, you should take time to read through your application forms. Any errors must be eliminated. A spelling or grammatical error in an application form could very possibly cost you the job – and all your efforts will have been wasted. If possible, ask a friend or family member to double-check for you.

Correcting errors is easy if you're completing your application form online. However, if you've made an error on your final copy of a paper-based form then you should correct it as neatly as possible, preferably using correction fluid.

Five top tips for application forms

Make an effort to take into account the following top tips when preparing your application form and you'll immediately be well above average.

1   **Read, think and plan.** Before you even consider putting pen to paper, make sure you have read carefully through any documents that accompany the application form – guidance notes, job description, person specification and so on. Ensure you also read right through the application form itself and that you fully understand all the questions.

2   **Get yourself into the right frame of mind.** Tedious it may be, but if you start writing your application form with a frown on your face then it's very likely to end up reflecting in your style of writing. Think positively, write positively and you stand a much better chance of making a positive impression on the reader. Sell yourself with enthusiasm.

3   **Bring your application form to life with real-world examples.** Wherever possible, you should try to integrate real-world examples into your statement rather than just speaking hypothetically. Flagging up specific, relevant examples from your own experience is an ideal way of reinforcing your points in the reader's mind.

4   **Check, double-check and check again.** Before submitting your application form, make sure you have checked every last sentence and that there aren't any spelling or grammatical errors. Sometimes it's hard to see the wood from the trees and a fresh pair of eyes – a friend or family member – can spot errors that you might have overlooked. You also want to be sure that you haven't missed a question.

5   **Keep a copy for future reference.** If you've got a paper-based
    application form then there's no excuse for not taking a photocopy
    once you've completed it. And even if you're completing the form
    online you should normally be able to print off what you've entered.
    If your application progresses to interview stage then you will
    definitely find it very useful to be able to refer back to what you said
    originally.

Further application form resources

Please visit the following page on The CV Centre's website for further help
with application forms: **http://www.ineedacv.co.uk/applicationforms**.

Job hunting

If you can, cast your mind back to the dark days before the invention of
the Internet ... Searching for a new job was definitely a lot more of an
uphill struggle back then, involving hours and hours scanning the jobs
pages, traipsing round recruitment agencies and posting off countless
letters to countless employers.

With the creation of the Internet (and email), life has undoubtedly
become a lot easier for a job hunter. However, whilst indeed very useful,
the Internet is only one aspect of a balanced job hunt. In order to maximise your chances of success, you will also need to take into account all
the more 'traditional' methods of finding a job.

In this section I will discuss the role the Internet should play in your job
hunt and I will also cover the other main options at your disposal.

The Internet

There is little doubt that the Internet is now the single most important
resource available to a job hunter. More and more employers are taking
advantage of the Internet to satisfy their
recruitment needs. It is therefore vital that you
make the Internet one of your first ports of call.

*make the internet one of
your first ports of call*

There are thousands and thousands of job sites
on the Web – some very general, some specialising in particular lines of work,
some specialising in recent graduates, some specialising in senior executives

and so on. (For links to specific resources please see the end of this section.) Both employers and recruitment agencies now make extensive use of such sites to advertise vacancies and to search for potential candidates.

Take the time to identify which job sites are most likely to be of use to you in your job hunt and then ensure you register with them and make the very most of what they have to offer. With so many sites out there, you could spend weeks going through them all, but I would recommend you be quite selective – there's probably only a dozen or so that really have the capacity to help you. However, it all depends on how much time you want to dedicate to this, because it's not going to cost you any more than your time – in almost all cases access is entirely free. It's the organisations advertising the vacancies and mining the database who provide the funding for these sites to operate.

The technology used by many sites is very sophisticated, enabling you to speedily locate vacancies that meet your specific requirements in terms of line of work, geographical area, salary range and so on. Other facilities include email alerts, where, having fed your criteria into the system, you will be automatically notified by email of any new vacancies that might be of interest to you. But these are just a couple of features; on most sites there are usually many more. Job sites are constantly in severe competition with each other and are always seeking to create and launch new facilities that will help their site users.

Whilst it definitely makes sense to concentrate on vacancies that have only recently been advertised (or for which the closing dates have not yet passed), it can be a surprisingly successful strategy to apply for older vacancies. There are many reasons why these vacancies might not yet have been filled – or might have been filled but the candidate didn't subsequently make it past their initial trial period.

As well as advertising vacancies on job sites, many employers will have their own websites that can include details of vacancies they currently have on offer. Larger employers may even provide facilities for you to submit your application immediately online – either by completing a brief form and attaching your CV and cover letter or by completing a full online application form.

Besides the above, all of the more 'traditional' methods of job hunting now have an online element – and I will talk about each of these in turn.

Recruitment agencies

Recruitment agencies are, in my professional opinion, second only to the Internet in terms of their importance to you in your job hunt.

Most recruitment agencies also have a Web presence, enabling you to quickly and efficiently locate the ones that might be appropriate for you. But I'd also recommend you have a quick look through your local *Yellow Pages* – because that should give you a good overview of the agencies located more or less on your own doorstep.

A successful recruitment consultant will have an in-depth knowledge of the local job market and useful contacts with key local employers. Recruitment consultants have a vested financial interest in helping you to locate the job you want so they are normally very committed to that task. Besides finding you a job they will be very keen to help you to secure that job. They don't get paid unless you actually win the job! They will there-fore be able to offer you a range of valuable advice, including helping you to negotiate your salary package.

You should aim to identify at least a handful of recruitment agencies that cater for candidates with backgrounds similar to your own. Then take the time to visit them in person. Like job sites, some recruitment agencies will specialise in particular sectors whilst others will be more general in their coverage; some will only handle permanent vacancies whilst others will also deal with temporary roles. Many recruitment agencies are small, local operations. However, there are a number of major national (and inter-national) chains and, if these cover your line of work, they should definitely be your primary target. They will typically have access to a much wider range of vacancies, not least because many employers will have an exclusive agreement with one agency – and only one.

Whilst there are undoubtedly many advantages to having a face-to-face meeting with a real, live human being – and many recruitment agencies will insist on this – you should note that there are an increasing number of recruitment agencies that operate principally online, taking advantage of the Internet to broaden their market and reduce their high street overhead. It would be a mistake to rule these out of your job search just because you're unable to meet with them in person.

Newspapers, magazines, journals, etc.

Even with the Internet at your fingertips, I'd strongly recommend you nevertheless take the time to trawl through newspapers (both local and national), magazines, trade journals and so on, which might contain job adverts of relevance to you.

Many jobseekers will be familiar with the process of flicking through the pages, circling possibilities and then short-listing vacancies for which you are actually going to apply. However, your life will be made easier by the fact that almost all publications now have websites with dedicated job sections. These will not only repeat most (if not all) of the adverts contained within the printed version of their publication, but they will also often carry additional adverts that only appear online.

The more prestigious publications are more likely to have more advanced websites, offering many of the same features as a major job site – sophisticated search facilities, email alerts and so on. It is, after all, in their interests for their advertisers to achieve a successful outcome – because it increases the chances of their paying for further advertising in the future.

Another facet of printed publications worth mentioning is that, apart from job adverts, they often contain a lot of useful background information on organisations. Even if an organisation isn't currently advertising a vacancy, you can make use of such information to submit a speculative application. Nothing ventured, nothing gained!

Networking

Networking is – and always has been – a valuable job-hunting technique. I hired someone just recently as a result of their applying through a mutual contact.

Networking takes many different forms and, for some people, it's almost an art form! It's also increasingly popular online with the advent of a wide range of social (and professional) networking sites.

Whatever means you use, if you are able to build up a network of contacts within your industry or sector, the information they can provide could be very useful to your job hunt.

Networking can help you to identify vacancies before they're even advertised, as well as help you to identify possible targets for speculative applications.

Job fairs

Whilst attending job and careers fairs can be time consuming, it can also be extremely productive. In the space of a few hours you could have the opportunity to talk face to face with recruiters from dozens of different employers.

There's a whole multitude of different job fairs – some industry-specific, some targeting graduates, some only dealing with senior executives and so on. Use the Internet to identify those that might be appropriate for you. Your local Job Centre should also be able to provide you with such information.

When attending a job fair, make sure you dress as if you were attending an interview.

brilliant blooper

I have seen too many jobseekers walking round summer job fairs wearing T-shirt, shorts and flip-flops!

Most importantly, make sure you take a plentiful supply of CVs with you. Don't just take your CV on a memory stick and expect the recruiter to be able to download it – take actual printed copies.

Visit as many (appropriate) stands as possible and, politely but firmly, make contact with the individuals manning them. You're unlikely to be formally interviewed on the spot; this is all about making an initial approach and then, subsequently, building on that relationship. It's very much a form of networking. Collect business cards as if your life depended on it! Taking a large folder (or briefcase) with you is also advisable so as to help you physically cope with the quantity of corporate literature that will inevitably be thrust your way.

It's a numbers game

If your CV and cover letters are only being received by a handful of people per week, it could be that you're not getting yourself enough exposure to have an impact. As advertised positions often attract over 100 applications, on average one might conclude you need to make over 100 applications to secure the position you want.

That sounds a lot but, in reality, provided you have a strong CV and cover letter, the odds should increase very much in your favour. However, I won't hide the fact that finding the *right* job will most definitely require some work. But it will be worth it!

Further job-hunting resources

Please visit the following page on The CV Centre's website for further job-hunting resources. It contains a range of useful links to job sites and other online resources. I keep the list online because that way I can keep it bang up to date at all times: **http://www.ineedacv.co.uk/resources**.

Interviews

Your application has been successful and you have been invited for interview. What next? People often think, well, I'll just turn up and be myself – which is fine, but it won't get you the job! You need to work hard to get yourself ready for an interview as you are still up against many other applicants – and this is your key opportunity to make an impact.

Planning, preparation and organisation: a winning strategy

The best person for the job, in terms of the right skills, experience and achievements, doesn't always pass the interview. The best person for the job doesn't always get the job. Sometimes the most able candidate on paper can really shoot themselves in the foot when they actually get to the interview.

> the best person for the job doesn't always get the job

The interview is one of the most critical points in the job search process. Whilst you might look great on paper, you need subsequently to prove that in front of a hiring manager. Many other factors that are not related to the person's ability to do the job are going to be picked up in the interview.

You've got the skills; now you need to demonstrate clearly that you'll be a good fit with your future co-workers and employers. It's so easy to sabotage this valuable opportunity if you're unprepared.

On average, there are likely to be at least five other candidates being interviewed for the same vacancy. So, everything else being equal, that gives you, at the most, a 20 per cent chance of getting the job. But there's so much you can do to improve your odds of success.

Pre-interview questionnaire

In order to help you plan and prepare for your interview I have developed the following brief questionnaire. It should help to get you thinking about all the most important issues you need to consider.

1 Regarding yourself and your interview history.

   (a) How many interviews have you attended within the past two years and how many of these have resulted in a job offer?

   (b) If any of your interviews failed to win you a job offer, why do you think that was?

   (c) What, if any, feedback have you received from an interviewer after an interview?

2 If you have won an interview for a specific role within a specific organisation.

   (a) Have you applied for a position at this organisation before and/or what previous knowledge or experience of the organisation do you have?

   (b) What is it about this particular position that appeals to you?

   (c) If this position marks a change in career direction for you then why have you decided to make this change?

   (d) What, if any, is your understanding/perception of the organisation's internal culture?

(e)   What, if any, further information do you have with regard to the kind of skills and experience the organisation is looking for?

(f)   Have you been asked to prepare a presentation, and if so, what instructions have you been given (e.g. content, time, visual aids to use, etc.)?

Interview scenarios: expecting the unexpected

There are so many different kinds of interview. Here are some of the possible scenarios with which you might be faced:

- Classic one-on-one interviews
- Panel interviews
- Competency-based interviews
- Psychometric and aptitude tests
- Presentations
- Group interviews
- Assessment centres
- Telephone, video-conferencing and webcams

Interview questions

Whilst there are of course thousands of possible questions you could be asked, it's most important that you prepare thoroughly for the following 'top 10'.

You should make sure you think through your answers to all these questions very carefully before getting anywhere near an interview room. Try to understand the meaning behind each question – what the interviewer's intentions are in asking you the question.

1   Tell me about your work experience. What did you do, what did you enjoy, what were you good at, why did you leave each job?

2   Why have you applied for this vacancy?

3   Why do you wish to leave your current position?

4   Why do you want to work for this organisation?

5   What are your strengths?

6   What are your weaknesses?

7   What has been your greatest achievement – in your personal life as well as in your career?

8   What can you, above all the other applicants, bring to this job?

9   Where do you see yourself in five years' time?

10   You've mentioned x under the interests and activities on your CV. Can you tell me a bit more about that?

You are absolutely certain to get asked at least some of these questions (or variations of them), if not the whole lot.

I could add an eleventh question to the list: 'And do you have any questions for me/us?' There aren't many interviews that conclude without this question being asked – so you'll need to make sure you think of some good questions of your own to ask the interviewer.

Five top tips to interview success

Make an effort to accommodate the following and you'll immediately be well above average.

1   **Be prepared.** The key to preventing pre-interview jitters is preparation. If you are going to convince a recruiter that you are right for the role then you obviously first need to get it clear in your own mind why you are right for the role. As well as researching the job itself, you should also research the organisation.

2   **Work through my pre-interview questionnaire.** I would recommend you take the time to complete the questionnaire above before any interview. It's only a short list of key questions, but it should really help to get you thinking in the right direction.

3   **Make sure you're there on time.** Yes, it may seem so obvious, yet late arrival is consistently one of the very top reasons cited by recruiters for their rejecting candidates at interview stage. Don't be late. Better than that, aim to get there early so as to have time to relax and compose yourself.

4   **Be confident and show your enthusiasm.** Confident people inspire confidence in others. If you appear confident that you are able to do the job, the employer is likely to be more inclined to believe that you can. Showing a lack of enthusiasm is generally fatal to your chances of success. Be enthusiastic – and show it. Confidence and enthusiasm are traits that are guaranteed to impress an interviewer.

> confident people inspire confidence in others

5   **Don't recite your answers parrot-fashion.** It's essential for you to think for yourself and to create your own answers to potential questions. Too many candidates make the mistake of sounding like they're reciting answers from an interview book. Even if you have prepared and memorised your own answers, you should be careful to make sure that your delivery is natural and doesn't come across as rehearsed.

The Interview Book

If you would like to learn more about interviews then please take a look at my comprehensive book on the subject, *The Interview Book*. You can place your order for a copy via the following page on The CV Centre website: **http://www.ineedacv.co.uk/theinterviewbook**.

CHAPTER 10

My five top tips to make your cover letter stand out

f you only have time to read one chapter of *Brilliant Cover Letters*, this is the one I would most like you to take the time to read. See it as a 'cheat sheet'. It encapsulates the most important principles that we have covered in the book. Make an effort to accommodate all these when writing your cover letter and you'll immediately be well above average.

1   **Get through to the right person**

The best person to whom to address your cover letter is the person who is going to be making the decision as to whether or not to interview you. Not only do letters addressed to a specific person achieve better results, but letters that actually reach the decision maker have an even higher chance of making the grade.

2   **Communicate clearly, concisely, engagingly and articulately**

It is essential for your letter to be easy for the reader to scan quickly and effectively. Take your time to carefully phrase your thoughts; do not rush yourself. Make sure you get your message across.

3   **Tell a good story**

Like all the best stories, the best letters have a strong – and clearly defined – beginning, middle and end. It's important to make sure your letter is structured in a logical fashion. Capture their attention, make an impact, maintain their interest and finish with a strong closing paragraph.

4   **Target/tailor your letter**

You should always tailor your letters according to the specific organisation to which you are applying. A carefully targeted letter can easily mean the difference between success and failure. Nobody likes being spammed.

5   **Check your spelling and your grammar**

Before sending off any letter, make sure you have read through it very carefully and that there are no spelling or grammatical errors. It's always a good idea to ask someone else to double-check for you.

Conclusion

Writing a cover letter is not rocket science! Most of what I have outlined is reasonably simple to take on board and it's just a matter of putting in the necessary time and effort.

I do hope you have found *Brilliant Cover Letters* useful. Don't forget to visit The CV Centre's online forum to let us know how you get on: **http://www.ineedacv.co.uk/forum**.

You will also have the opportunity to make contact with me and my team directly.

Good luck!

Further reading and resources

Recommended books

Borg, J. (2007) *Persuasion: The Art of Influencing People*, 2nd edn, Harlow: Prentice Hall

Borg, J. (2008) *Body Language: 7 Easy Lessons to Master the Silent Language*, Harlow: Prentice Hall Life

Bright, J. and Earl, J. (2008) *Brilliant CV*, 3rd edn, Harlow: Prentice Hall Business

Edenborough, R. (2009) *Brilliant Psychometric Tests*, Harlow: Prentice Hall Business

Fagan, A. (2007) *Brilliant Job Hunting*, 2nd edn, Harlow: Prentice Hall Business

Faust, B. and Faust, M. (2006) *Pitch Yourself*, 2nd edn, Harlow: Prentice Hall Business

Hall, R. (2008) *The Secrets of Success at Work: 10 Steps to Accelerating Your Career*, Harlow: Prentice Hall Business

Hodgson, S. (2007) *Brilliant Tactics to Pass Aptitude Tests*, 2nd edn, Harlow: Prentice Hall Business

Hodgson, S. (2008) *Brilliant Answers to Tough Interview Questions*, 3rd edn, Harlow: Prentice Hall Business

Innes, J. (2009) *The CV Book*, Harlow: Prentice Hall

Innes, J. (2009) *The Interview Book*, Harlow: Prentice Hall

Jay, R. (2008) *Brilliant Interview*, 2nd edn, Harlow: Prentice Hall Business

Johnson, S. (2007) *Brilliant Word 2007*, Harlow: Prentice Hall Business

Perkins, G. (2007) *Killer CVs & Hidden Approaches*, 3rd edn, Harlow: Prentice Hall Business

Taylor, N. (2008) *Brilliant Business Writing*, Harlow: Prentice Hall Business

Templar, R. (2002) *The Rules of Work: A Definitive Guide to Personal Success*, Harlow: Prentice Hall Business

Yeung, R. (2008) *Confidence: The Art of Getting Whatever You Want*, Harlow: Prentice Hall Life

These titles are available from all major bookshops. You can also learn more about them and even place an order for a copy by visiting the following page on The CV Centre's website:
http://www.ineedacv.co.uk/recommendedbooks3.

Online resources

I keep my list of online resources – online. That way I can keep it bang up to date at all times. Please access the following page for a wide range of useful links to job sites and other online resources: **http://www.ineedacv.co.uk/resources**.

Appendix A: 250 action verbs

Accomplished
Achieved
Acquired
Administered
Advised
Advocated
Analysed
Anticipated
Appointed
Appraised
Approved
Arbitrated
Arranged
Articulated
Assembled
Assessed
Assisted
Attained
Audited
Augmented
Authorised
Averted
Avoided

Balanced
Began
Bought
Briefed
Budgeted
Built

Calculated
Captured

Centralised
Changed
Clarified
Classified
Coached
Collated
Collected
Combined
Communicated
Completed
Composed
Compounded
Conceived
Conducted
Conserved
Consolidated
Constructed
Consulted
Contributed
Controlled
Converted
Convinced
Coordinated
Corrected
Corresponded
Counselled
Created
Criticised

Dealt
Debated
Decided
Decreased

Defined
Delegated
Delivered
Demonstrated
Designated
Designed
Detected
Determined
Developed
Devised
Diagnosed
Diminished
Directed
Discovered
Dispensed
Disproved
Distributed
Documented
Doubled
Dropped

Earned
Edited
Educated
Effected
Elected
Eliminated
Employed
Enabled
Encouraged
Enforced
Engineered
Enjoyed

Ensured
Established
Estimated
Evaluated
Examined
Exceeded
Executed
Expanded
Expedited
Explained
Explored
Extracted

Facilitated
Forecast
Formed
Formulated
Fostered
Founded
Functioned

Gained
Galvanised
Gathered
Generated
Guided

Handled
Heightened
Highlighted
Hired

Identified
Implemented
Improved
Improvised
Increased
Initiated
Inspected
Inspired
Installed
Instigated
Instituted
Instructed

Interacted
Introduced
Invented
Investigated

Launched
Led
Liaised
Liquidated
Located
Logged

Maintained
Managed
Mapped
Marketed
Maximised
Mediated
Modernised
Modified
Monitored
Motivated

Named
Navigated
Negotiated
Networked

Observed
Obtained
Operated
Ordered
Organised
Originated
Oversaw

Participated
Perceived
Performed
Pioneered
Placed
Planned
Positioned
Prepared

Prescribed
Presented
Prevailed
Prevented
Prioritised
Processed
Procured
Produced
Profited
Programmed
Promoted
Protected
Proved
Provided
Published
Purchased

Raised
Ran
Rated
Realised
Received
Recognised
Recommended
Reconciled
Recorded
Recruited
Redesigned
Reduced
Referred
Regulated
Rejected
Related
Rendered
Reorganised
Represented
Researched
Resolved
Restored
Reviewed
Revised
Revitalised
Routed

Saved	Standardised	Terminated
Scheduled	Stimulated	Tested
Scrutinised	Streamlined	Tightened
Selected	Strengthened	Traded
Sent	Studied	Trained
Served	Supervised	Transformed
Settled	Supplied	Tripled
Shaped	Supported	
Simplified	Surpassed	Vitalised
Sold	Surveyed	
Solved		Wrote
Specified	Targeted	
Staffed	Taught	

Appendix B: 50 positive adjectives

Able
Accurate
Adaptable
Analytical
Articulate
Astute

Consistent
Creative

Decisive
Dedicated
Diligent
Diplomatic
Dynamic

Effective
Efficient
Energetic
Enthusiastic
Experienced

Fast
Flexible

Gregarious

Imaginative
Innovative
Inventive

Methodical
Motivated

Organised
Outgoing
Outstanding

Patient
Perceptive
Persistent
Positive
Practical
Productive

Proficient
Punctual

Quick

Rational
Reliable
Resourceful
Responsible

Self-motivated
Self-reliant
Shrewd
Strong
Successful

Tactful
Talented

Versatile

Index